Christmas Gifts That Won't Break
Expanded Edition with Devotions

Christmas Gifts That Won't Break

Christmas Gifts That Won't Break: Expanded Edition with Devotions
978-1-5018-3998-6 Book • 978-1-5018-3999-3 ePub
978-1-5018-4000-5 Large Print

Christmas Gifts That Won't Break: Leader Guide
978-1-5018-4001-2 Book • 978-1-5018-4002-9 ePub

Christmas Gifts That Won't Break: DVD
978-1-5018-4003-6

Christmas Gifts That Won't Break: Youth Study Book
978-1-5018-4004-3 Book • 978-1-5018-4005-0 ePub

Christmas Gifts That Won't Break: Children's Leader Book
978-1-5018-4006-7

Also by James W. Moore

Yes Lord, I Have Sinned, But I Have Several Excellent Excuses
Lord, Give Me Patience, and Give It to Me Right Now!
How God Takes Our Little and Makes It Much
If God Is Your Co-pilot, Swap Seats!
Have You Ever Seen a Hearse Pulling a Trailer?
Some Things Are Too Good Not to Be True
If God Has a Refrigerator, Your Picture Is on It
You Can Get Bitter or Better!
Standing on the Promises or Sitting on the Premises?
Healing Where It Hurts
Moments That Take Your Breath Away
God Was Here and I Was Out to Lunch
Are You Fired Up or Burned Out?
The Power of a Story
Finding Bethlehem in the Midst of Bedlam

Also by Jacob Armstrong

The Connected Life	Treasure
Renovate	Loving Large
Sent	Upside Down
The New Adapters	The God Story

James W. Moore

with Jacob Armstrong

CHRISTMAS GIFTS
That Won't Break

Expanded Edition with Devotions

Abingdon Press
Nashville

CHRISTMAS GIFTS THAT WON'T BREAK
Expanded Edition with Devotions

978-1-5018-3998-6

Scripture quotations are taken from the Common English Bible, copyright 2011. Used by permission. All rights reserved.

Scripture quotations marked (NIV) are taken from the Holy Bible, New International Version®, NIV®. Copyright © 1973, 1978, 1984, 2011 by Biblica, Inc.˙ Used by permission of Zondervan. All rights reserved worldwide. www.zondervan.com The "NIV" and "New International Version" are trademarks registered in the United States Patent and Trademark Office by Biblica, Inc.™

Scripture quotations marked NLT are taken from the Holy Bible, New Living Translation, copyright © 1996, 2004, 2007. Used by permission of Tyndale House Publishers, Inc., Carol Stream, Illinois 60188. All rights reserved.

Scripture quotations marked NRSV are taken from the New Revised Standard Version of the Bible, copyright 1989, Division of Christian Education of the National Council of the Churches of Christ in the United States of America. Used by permission. All rights reserved.

Cover Design: Marcia Myatt

17 18 19 20 21 22 23 24 25 26 — 10 9 8 7 6 5 4 3 2 1
MANUFACTURED IN THE UNITED STATES OF AMERICA

CONTENTS

INTRODUCTION

Bishop Kenneth Shamblin once told a story about something that happened to his son, Ken Jr., on Christmas afternoon. Ken Jr. was about five years old at the time, and more than anything he wanted a red toy truck for Christmas that year. That's all he could talk about. He told his parents. He pointed it out to them at the toy store. He showed them a picture of it in the catalog. He wrote to Santa. He went to the mall to tell Santa in person how much he wanted that particular red toy truck for Christmas. He even prayed about it.

Then, on Christmas morning, there it was under the tree. Ken Jr. was overjoyed! He received many other presents, but he hardly noticed them. All of his five-year-old attention was riveted on that bright, shiny, new red toy truck. For so long he had dreamed about it, and now his dream was reality.

All morning long he played with it. But then, shortly after Christmas dinner, Bishop Shamblin had just sat down in the den to read the newspaper when he heard his son crying. He laid the paper aside, and there was Ken Jr. standing in front of him. In his right hand Ken Jr. held the red toy truck, and in his left hand he held the wheels. Through tears he said, "Daddy, my Christmas is broken already!"

Now, I am happy to report that the red toy truck was fixed pretty quickly. But for me, that episode raises an interesting question: *What are the Christmas gifts that won't break?*

Jesus said something that might help us answer that question. He said, "Stop collecting treasures for your own benefit on earth, where moth and rust eat them and where thieves break in and steal them. Instead, collect treasures for yourselves in heaven. . . . Where your treasure is, there your heart will be also" (Matthew 6:19-21). Jesus was giving us a much-needed warning. He was saying, "Be careful now. Don't get your heart too set on material things. Material things aren't permanent. They wear out, they break, they erode, they go out of fashion, they can be lost or stolen. Material things are nice, but don't get too attached to them. Rather, build your happiness on things you cannot lose, on things that are independent of the chances and the changes of life."

The great poet Robert Burns once wrote a poem about how fleeting things can be and how quickly they can get away from us. He wrote:

> But pleasures are like poppies spread,
> You seize the flow'r, its bloom is shed;
> Or like the snow falls in the river,
> A moment white—then melts forever.
> –"Tam o' Shanter" [1790]

Any one of us whose life and happiness depends on material things will surely be disappointed, because material things do not last. They go out of style. They wear out. They break.

So during this Advent season, I want us to think together about Christmas gifts that won't break. There are many, of course, but in this four-week season we will focus on the four gifts represented by the four outer candles of the traditional Advent wreath: hope, love, joy, and peace. And in a fifth chapter, corresponding to Christmas Day, we will explore the gift symbolized by the Christ candle in the center: the gift of Jesus Christ, the gift of God's Son.

It is my prayer that as we go through this Advent season together, we might—as never before—receive from God and then pass on to others the Christmas gifts that won't break.

Chapter One

THE GIFT OF HOPE

1

THE GIFT OF HOPE

This is how the birth of Jesus Christ took place. When Mary his mother was engaged to Joseph, before they were married, she became pregnant by the Holy Spirit. Joseph her husband was a righteous man. Because he didn't want to humiliate her, he decided to call off their engagement quietly. As he was thinking about this, an angel from the Lord appeared to him in a dream and said, "Joseph son of David, don't be afraid to take Mary as your wife, because the child she carries was conceived by the Holy Spirit. She will give birth to a son, and you will call him Jesus, because he will save his people from their sins."

Matthew 1:18-21

Some years ago our family gathered in Winston-Salem, North Carolina, for the wedding of our nephew. I reserved a room at a local hotel with two double beds, so our daughter Jodi and granddaughter Sarah could share the room with us. Sarah was five years old at the time, and we never knew what she was going to say next.

After the first night at the hotel, I asked Sarah if she had slept well. She said, "Well, Gran, let me explain it like this. At my dayschool we take naps after lunch. But there is a boy in my class named Tyler who snores and I can't get any rest." She paused for a moment, then said, "I think Tyler was in our room last night."

Now, according to Matthew 1 there wasn't a Tyler in the room that night with Joseph, but there was an angel, and after his encounter with the angel, Joseph probably didn't get much rest either! Remember the story with me.

Joseph and Mary were engaged and going through the traditional year of betrothal before their formal marriage could take place. They had not had the wedding ceremony yet, were not living together, and had not been physically intimate, but in the eyes of the community they were as good as married. Then, out of the blue, Joseph received word that Mary was expecting! Joseph surely was shaken and heartsick. But he was a kind man and loved Mary, so he decided that instead of publicly humiliating her, he would just break it off quietly.

As Joseph was making his decision, an angel appeared to him in a dream and said words to this effect: "Joseph, don't be afraid. Go ahead and take Mary for your wife. Your love for each other is unique and special. The Spirit is with her bringing a new life. The child is of God. It is God's will that she will bear a son, and you shall call his name Jesus, for he will save his people from their sins."

In the Bible, angels are messengers from God, so imagine the powerful effect of this message of hope. The angel told

Joseph not to be afraid and not to abandon Mary, but instead to go ahead and marry her. The angel told Joseph that Mary would give birth to the Savior. And the angel told Joseph to name the baby Jesus. Don't miss this, now: the angel told Joseph what to name the baby!

There are so many remarkable images and lessons in this powerful section of Scripture, but for now let's focus in on the naming of the baby and what it says to us about the gift of hope.

Names Are Important

Have you noticed that people tend to live up—or down—to their names?

I know a man named Smiley. That is his legal name, and it is the ideal name for him because he smiles all the time. Even when he is experiencing life's tough moments, his face has a bright and gracious expression.

I know a man named Happy, and he is one of the happiest people I know.

I also have a good friend named Skippy, and he just "skips" through life with grace and charm and energy.

A woman I know is named Sunny, and the name fits her perfectly. She not only has beautiful blond hair that just glows, but her face is radiant and she has a golden disposition that is warm and wonderful. I have often wondered, *What if her parents had named her Stormy?* Would she be the same person? Or would she be different?

Then there is John Wesley Dowling, who turned out to be one of the finest Methodists I have ever known.

I'm sure there are exceptions, but more often than not people do indeed live up (or down) to their names. So, parents, be very careful when naming your children! That name can have a dramatic effect on the development of their personalities. Our children may well become what we name them.

The importance of names is a powerful and significant theme in the Bible. The Interpreter's Dictionary of the Bible puts it like this: "The giving of personal names in ancient Israel was not merely for the purpose of providing a distinctive label for an individual, but was also commonly (an occasion) for expressing religious convictions associated with the birth of a child or its future." (Interpreter's Dictionary of the Bible Supplementary Volume, 619).

For example, the name Elijah means "the Lord is my God." It's probably no accident that Elijah grew up to be a courageous prophet who called upon his people to worship Yahweh alone and not to bow down to Baal or the other gods of the Canaanite religion.

The name Moses was also fitting. It literally means "draw out." You probably remember that, as a baby, Moses was saved from being murdered. The Egyptian king, afraid that the Hebrew slaves might grow strong enough to rebel, had ordered for all Hebrew newborn baby boys to be killed. But the family of Moses came up with a creative plan to save his life. They put baby Moses into a basket and placed it among the reeds in the Nile River. The pharaoh's daughter found the baby, "drew him up out of the water," and adopted him. Later, you remember, Moses led the people of Israel through the parted waters of the Reed Sea, drawing them out of Egypt to save them. So Moses was indeed a good name for him.

In the New Testament, one of my favorite characters is Barnabas, whose name means "child of encouragement," which is exactly what he was.

Now, we notice also in the Scriptures that when something dramatic happened to change a person's life, in effect giving

"How do you feel about staying in power?"

them a new birth, their names were often changed to fit their new life. For example, after their covenant with God was made, Abram became Abraham and Sarai became Sarah. After he wrestled with the angel, Jacob became Israel. And Jesus changed Simon's name to Peter, *Petros*, "the rock."

And that brings us to the passage in Matthew 1.

THE NAMING OF THE CHRIST CHILD

The angel said to Joseph: "don't be afraid to take Mary as your wife, because the child she carries was conceived by the Holy Spirit. She will give birth to a son, and you will call him Jesus, because he will save his people from their sins" (Matthew 1:20-21). This announcement is the Christmas hope in a nutshell. It means that God will always be with us—watching over us, reconciling us, and saving us in this world and the world to come.

There is a gospel song that says it like this: "Jesus, Jesus, Jesus...There is something about that name." Indeed there is. The name *Jesus* means "savior" or "the lord's helper." But also notice—don't miss this now—that the name Jesus is the Greek form of the Hebrew name Joshua.

You remember, of course, who Joshua was. As the spiritual tells us, "Joshua fit the battle of Jericho. . . and the walls come tumblin' down." So we can also understand the name *Jesus* to mean "wall-breaker."

Here is how the apostle Paul expressed it in his Letter to the Ephesians, in one of the most powerful statements in all the Bible: "Christ is our peace. He made both Jews and Gentiles into one group. With his body, he broke down the barrier of hatred that divided us. . . . So now you are no longer strangers and aliens. Rather, you are fellow citizens with God's people, and you belong to God's household. As God's household, you are built on the foundation of the apostles and prophets with Christ Jesus himself as the cornerstone" (2:14, 19-20).

Now, this idea of Jesus being the wall-breaker, breaking down the dividing walls of hostility, can better be understood when we see it against the backdrop of the Temple's physical layout in the time of Jesus. The Temple was a parable in stone, exposing the prejudices, or walls, that existed in society during biblical times—walls that included a few privileged people but excluded or shut out most. As worshipers moved through the Temple toward the high altar (the Holy of Holies), they encountered a series of walls holding the people back from God.

The first wall held back foreigners, people of other races and nations. The second wall held back women. The third wall held back all men except the priests. The fourth wall, a veil surrounding the Holy of Holies, held back everyone except the High Priest, who was permitted to go inside the veil only once a year on the Day of Atonement. Even then the other priests tied a rope around his ankle, so that if he fell or passed out, they could pull him back without going inside!

The Holy of Holies, which represented the presence of God, was remote, fearsome, austere, and unapproachable. But then came Jesus, and he broke down the dividing walls and made us one. He brought God out to the people.

When you think of it, that's what Christmas is about: God breaking out, God smashing down the walls, God coming warmly and wonderfully into our lives. And when we forget about Christmas, when we neglect the teachings of Christ, then once again we start building up those walls, fostering hostility and hatred, prejudice and bigotry.

The walls we build today are every bit as real as those in the Temple. Here are some of them:

There are the walls that divide nations. However, Christ came as the Prince of Peace, the Savior of all people, and the Lord of all nations.

There are the walls that divide men and women. The truth is that Christ was the first real liberator of women. Read his teachings, study the Gospels, see how he respected women and included them, and notice how much he advanced the cause of equal rights and equal opportunity.

There are the walls that divide clergy and laity. Jesus made no such distinction. He sent all of the disciples out as ministers.

There are the walls that hold people back from God. More than anything, Jesus brought God to people and people to God. Jesus came not to change God's mind but to reveal it. He came to show us how much God loves us and how available God is to us.

Do you remember what happened in the Temple when Jesus was on the cross? The veil around the Holy of Holies was torn apart, from top to bottom. God did it! God tore it! God broke down that wall!

JESUS LIVED UP TO HIS NAME

Here is the good news of Christmas: Christ is our Savior, our Redeemer, and our Reconciler. He makes us all one. He breaks down the dividing walls and shows us that we are God's family. And that is our hope for peace on earth and good will toward all people.

This profound truth is captured in a story that was written by an American journalist who had to spend one Christmas Eve with his family in Paris. He writes that his family's entire trip had been one frustration after another, and they had to settle for a Christmas Eve dinner at a rundown restaurant.

There they found a local flower woman who had no customers, German and French families who looked as frustrated as his own, and one American sailor writing a letter home. They had all but lost their Christmas spirit, but then:

> The young sailor finished his meal and got up to leave. Putting on his coat, he walked over to the flower woman's table. "Happy Christmas," he said, smiling and picking out two corsages....
>
> Pressing one of the small corsages flat, he put it into the letter he had written, then handed the woman a twenty franc note.
>
> "I don't have change, monsieur," she said....
>
> "No, ma'am," said the sailor..."This is my Christmas present to you."
>
> Straightening up, he came to our table...."Sir," he said to me, "may I have permission to present these flowers to your beautiful daughter?" In one quick motion he gave my wife the corsage, wished us a merry Christmas, and departed.
>
> Everyone had stopped eating. Everyone had been watching the sailor. Everyone was silent. A few seconds later, Christmas exploded throughout the restaurant like a bomb. The old flower woman jumped up....The piano player began to belt out "Good King Wenceslaus"....My wife [sang]...and our three sons joined her, bellowing the song with uninhibited enthusiasm.
>
> "Gut! Gut!" shouted the Germans. They jumped on their chairs and began singing the words in German. The waiter embraced the flower woman. Waving their arms, they sang in French....

People crowded in from the street until many customers were standing....

The miserable evening in a shoddy restaurant ended up being the very best Christmas Eve we had ever experienced just because of a young sailor who had Christmas spirit in his soul. He released the love and joy that had been smothered within us by anger and disappointment. He gave us Christmas.

—William J. Lederer,
"A Sailor's Christmas Gift," *Chicken Soup for the Christian Soul* (Deerfield Beach, FL.: Health Communications, Inc., 1997), 320–21

His name shall be called Jesus the wall-breaker. He will save the people from their sins. Christ is the hope of the world. And hope is a Christmas gift that won't break!

DISCUSSION QUESTIONS

1. What does Advent mean to you? Why is it important? What do you hope to receive from participating in this small-group experience?

2. Discuss the encounter of Joseph and the angel. What feelings do you think Joseph experienced?

3. Why are names important? Discuss some of the ways in which names are chosen. Describe how and why you received your name.

4. List and discuss the meanings of the name Jesus. Why do you think this name is appropriate?

5. In what ways was Jesus considered a wall-breaker during his ministry?

6. In what ways does Jesus represent the gift of hope?

PRAYER

Dear God, thank you for the season of Advent and the gift of hope. Help us to prepare our hearts for your coming and to remember the true meaning of Christmas. Amen.

FOCUS FOR THE WEEK

Begin your observance of Advent by becoming an instrument of hope to others this week. Give the gift of hope to those who need it by giving of yourself. As Christmas draws near, look for opportunities to become a messenger of good news.

JOSEPH ACTUALLY
SAID SOMETHING

Matthew 1:18-25

Shea Glover, a high school student at the Chicago High School for the Arts, posted a video from a school project on YouTube in 2015. It now has millions of views. In the video, Shea stands behind the camera and prepares to take a video of her classmates, one at a time. Then as she begins to film, she explains the premise of her project. The premise, she says, is to film things she finds beautiful.

What happened next was not Shea's intent, but it quickly became the focus of the project and the reason it went viral. Shea's initial hope was to simply record beautiful people in her school. What the video became is a look at the stark difference between people's faces before and after they are told they are beautiful.

The reactions range from being embarrassed to being flattered. Some laugh or look away. One student angrily protests, thinking it a mean joke. Most, though, simply smile, showing an incredible before-and-after transformation.

Being called beautiful changes the way we look. Being called beautiful gives a gift we don't see coming. Words have power.

No one disputes that what we do is important. "Actions speak louder than words," we have heard, and in most cases that is true. What we see in the Advent Scriptures, though, is that what we say is really important, too. We hold the power to give a gift by what we say to people, about people, and about ourselves.

Joseph is one of the great characters in the story of Jesus' birth. Most people have heard of him. Mary gets a little more press—OK a lot more—but Joseph hangs right in there. We know Joseph is noble. We know that Joseph is a person of action, and with few exceptions it seems, the right action. What is striking, though, is that Joseph is a man of very few words. It is commonly observed that we don't know anything that Joseph said. Of course, no one thinks that Joseph didn't talk. It's just that there is no record of any of his words.

But, that's not quite true. Joseph said something. And we know what it is. Are you on the edge of your seat? One word. There is one recorded word from Joseph: *Jesus*.

After learning that his fiancée is pregnant, Joseph is told in a dream to not be afraid. An angel tells him to believe what Mary says is true. And Joseph is told to name the boy Jesus. The name means "savior," or as we learned, in a sense it means "wall-breaker." Joseph was told to name his son Savior, Deliverer, Wall-Breaker.

Joseph woke up from his dream and took Mary home as his wife. And we don't know when he named the baby. We don't know if it was when the baby was born in the middle of the night in a place where animals were kept in Bethlehem. We don't know if it was on the eighth day when the baby was ceremonially presented in the temple. But somewhere in there, Joseph names the baby Jesus. It's not exactly a direct quote attributed to Joseph, but it's clear that Joseph stated the child's name (Matthew 1:25). Jesus. This boy's name is Deliverer. My son's name, Joseph says, is Jesus, Savior, Wall-Breaker.

What we do is really important, and Joseph is mostly known for what he did. A study of Joseph is a study in what to do and really in what to do when times are hard. If you are facing something difficult right now, I commend Joseph to you. Joseph is the picture of doing the right God-thing when there are a ton of easier options. Joseph takes Mary home as his wife when he could have let her face public punishment. Joseph marries his fiancée when she said she had conceived a child by the Holy Spirit. Joseph faces ridicule and shame. Joseph loads Mary up on a donkey and takes a long journey with a nine-months pregnant wife with no place to stay at the end of the trip. Joseph travels with Mary and the child Jesus to Egypt to live as refugees running for their lives from a tyrannical government. Joseph is known for what he did. But what I want to propose to you today is that what he said may have been just as important.

Joseph did say something. I'm sure he said a lot. I'm sure he and Mary had to talk through that whole Holy Spirit–conception thing. I'm sure they shared some special words as they wrapped their baby in swaddling clothes. I'm sure they prayed fear-filled prayers as they escaped to Egypt in the night. But all we know for sure that he said is this: "Jesus."

He gave the name to the Son of God.

Why is that important? Because what we call people can make all the difference.

"You are beautiful," Shea Glover said.

I still remember some names I was called as a kid. "Four Eyes" was the greeting I received in third grade on my first day at school with new glasses. And then that same morning, when I sat down at my desk, my teacher, Ms. Lowe, greeted me with, "Cool Glasses." I'll let you guess which one I chose to believe.

What we call people could be the most important gift we can give. Old man-of-a-few-words Joseph, when his son was born, basically said, "His name is Jesus," and it may have been the most significant name calling in human history.

We are called to speak that name into our world. Jesus. God saves. God delivers. God will rescue us. God will do whatever it takes to break down walls. Christians believe a crazy thing. We believe that there is power in the name of Jesus. Just like Joseph, who believed a crazy thing, we believe some crazy things connected to the name of Jesus.

Jesus' name brings the gift of hope for healing. Peter and John said, "Stretch out your hand to bring healing and enable signs and wonders to be performed through the name of Jesus, your holy servant" (Acts 4:30). James said that the elders of the church should pray for healing in the name of the Lord Jesus (James 5:14). Recently in the hallway of a children's hospital, I prayed in the name of Jesus for the healing of a little boy. We do it all the time. We believe that in Jesus' powerful name is found the gift of hope for healing.

Jesus' name brings the gift of hope for refuge. We believe that in times we are afraid, times we are at war, and times we find ourselves refugees in foreign lands that there is hope in Jesus. Our ancient proverbs tell us that "the Lord's name is a strong tower; the righteous run to it and find refuge" (Proverbs 18:10). The prophet Zephaniah called out to an exiled people to "seek refuge in the name of the Lord" (Zephaniah 3:12). There is hope for refuge in the name of Jesus.

Jesus' name brings the gift of hope for deliverance. Jesus' disciples will throw out demons in his name (Mark 16:17). Those who boldly go out to share the hope found in Jesus find this power (Luke 10:17). There are some things that only Jesus' name can cast out.

Jesus' name brings the gift of hope for salvation. Everyone who calls on his name will be saved (Acts 4:12; Romans 10:13). We are saved by calling on the name of Jesus and the first guy to say it was Joseph. He may not have said much, but what he said was important.

The Advent Scriptures show us the gift of hope found in the name of Jesus, but also the power that his name has to change what we hear about ourselves. Encountering Jesus is not just about hearing his name, but it is also about hearing our names spoken in a different way. All the characters in the story of Jesus coming into the world as a baby find that what they are called has new meaning because of Jesus.

My name is Forgotten. Surely no one felt as forgotten as Zechariah and Elizabeth. They were nearing the end of their careers and past child-bearing age when God surprised them with the announcement of their son, John. Surely they felt forgotten. Zechariah received this news with this address: "Don't be afraid, Zechariah" (Luke 1:13). Zechariah's name means "The Lord Remembered." The announcement of John's arrival, which ushered in Jesus' arrival, surely was a way for Zechariah to hear his name in a new way. **Your name is Remembered.** How do you feel forgotten? Perhaps this Advent is God's time for you to hear that you are remembered.

My name is Bitter. Mary's name in Hebrew means "bitter." Yep, what has become perhaps the most popular female name of all time means bitter (see Ruth 1:20). Well, at least it did. When Mary received the news that Jesus was coming into her life, when she learned that the Wall-Breaker would dwell in her, she sang, "From now on, everyone will consider me highly favored" (Luke 1:48). And she was right. After Mary encountered Jesus, her name would never mean bitter again. Her name means "blessed."

30

Maybe you have some bitterness today. You've had enough and you've tried to stay strong. One person can only take so much. Like Mary, perhaps your bitterness is not just your own, but you represent a whole line of folks for whom it hasn't gone the way you hoped. You've been waiting for God to bail you out and God hasn't shown up. What if God could change everything with the announcement of God's Son? What if you receive the news that, in your own way, you will carry God's Son in you? **Your name is Blessed.** God has something good for you, good in you, good that God wants to do in you and through you.

My name is I Don't Have Enough. There are many of us who would simply say, "I don't have enough." I don't have enough money, enough time, enough energy, maybe not enough compassion. Joseph had to feel that way. I don't have enough, God, to do this crazy thing you are asking me to do. I do not have enough strength, enough courage, or enough faith. But then Joseph hears God call his name. Before he is naming anybody, he has to hear God say his name. Joseph's name means "The Lord will add." Joseph's name actually means that God will give more.

God wants to speak that to you today. There is more. **Your name is The Lord Will Increase.** You are right, you don't have enough. You can't do this on your own. But God will give you more.

And in the event you need to hear what the students at the Chicago High School for the Arts needed to hear, you don't have to go watch YouTube. God has something to say to you.

31

Your name is Beautiful. You are beautiful. You are made by God. You are made in the image of God. You are made in the love of God and you are made to love like God.

And as we receive the gift of hope in our new names, we speak it to others.

So today, tell some people who think they are ugly that they are beautiful. You are telling the truth. They were made in the image of God. Watch them change.

Tell someone who is bitter that she is blessed. You aren't lying. Every person is a child of God and a blessed person of worth.

Tell someone who thinks he is forgotten that he is indeed remembered by you.

Tell someone who is tired and doesn't have enough that God's strength is available to her.

God is sending you in Jesus' name.

The only thing we know Joseph to have said is "Jesus." When the baby was born he looked at him, the Son of God in flesh, and said "Jesus." It is the name by which one day every knee will bow. It is the name that sends demons scurrying away to dark places.

Thank God for Joseph who said the name "Jesus" and brought the gift of hope to the world.

Day 1

As we read Joseph's story, we see the gift of hope throughout. God offers hope on a very personal level to Joseph, but also in a big way as hope will come to the whole world through the Christ Child. As you journey through this day, be mindful of the places where you may have lost hope. Remember that Jesus is coming into your life and even more than that Jesus is coming into the world. If you begin to feel cynicism, despair, or a loss of hope, think about Joseph, think about Jesus.

Day 2

Jesus' name means "He is a Wall-Breaker." We know that means that Jesus brought down the walls that separate us from God, conquering sin and death. As you receive that promise, consider also what other walls you have put up in your life. What walls need to come down? What is necessary for that to happen? The same Spirit that conquered sin and death now lives in you.

Day 3

Actions speak louder than words, but words are important, too! Your words hold power. You have the power to speak blessings over others. As you see others, think about how they might look at themselves. Perhaps they have accepted names for themselves that are not true. How can you give someone a new name?

Day 4

We have pondered the power that is found in Jesus' name. In his name is the power to heal, guard, deliver, and save. What action is God calling you to that will usher Jesus' name into a situation, a relationship, or an injustice? Is there something you can do today that will usher in the name of Jesus?

Day 5

Joseph's name means "The Lord Will Add." Surely Joseph felt at times that he didn't have enough. Surely, there are times you feel that way. What do you need God to add to you today? Remember that Jesus says his grace is sufficient for you. His strength is made perfect in your weakness. God adds to us oftentimes not by taking away our deficiencies, but by God's strength being magnified in our weakness.

Day 6

We hear many different voices and many different messages in the course of a day. As you go through your day, pause to consider what you are hearing and who is speaking. Seek to be able to distinguish between lies and the truth. What are some lies that have been spoken over you? What would it look like for you to seek to hear God's voice today?

Day 7

As we close this week, where we have marveled over God's gift of hope to us through Jesus, think of an intentional way that you can share hope. Look for an opportunity where you can share hope with the hopeless. In doing so, you will be a part of the story of Christ's coming.

Chapter Two

THE GIFT OF LOVE

2

THE GIFT OF LOVE

*When the angels returned to heaven, the shepherds
said to each other, "Let's go right now to Bethlehem
and see what's happened. Let's confirm what the
Lord has revealed to us." They went quickly and
found Mary and Joseph, and the baby lying in the
manger. When they saw this, they reported what they
had been told about this child. Everyone who heard it
was amazed at what the shepherds told them. Mary
committed these things to memory and considered
them carefully. The shepherds returned home,
glorifying and praising God for all they had heard and
seen. Everything happened just as they had been told.*

Luke 2:15-20

Christmas is a time for the telling of stories. Wonderful,
heart-warming stories cluster beautifully around Christmas.

Here is one of my favorites. Written by M. A. Matthews, it is called "The Gift of a Child."

> The day was frightfully cold,...with swirls of snow in the air, and I was looking out the living room window...which faces our church. Workmen had just finished constructing the annual Nativity scene in the church-yard...when school let out for the day. Children gathered excitedly around the crèche,...but they didn't stay long; it was far too cold for lingering. All the children took a quick look at the manger scene and then hurried away—except for a tiny girl of about six.
>
> The wind lashed at her bare legs and caused her coat to fly open in the front...but she was oblivious of the weather. She was captivated by that manger scene. All her attention was riveted on the statues before her. Which one I couldn't tell. Was it Mary? The baby? The shepherds? The Wise Men? The animals? I wondered!
>
> And then a beautiful and poignant moment... I saw her remove her blue woolen head scarf. The wind quickly knotted her hair into a wild tangle, but she didn't seem to notice that either. She had only one thought. Lovingly, she wrapped her scarf around the statue of the Baby Jesus. After she had covered it, she patted the baby and then kissed Him on the cheek. Satisfied, she skipped on down the street, her hair frosted with tiny diamonds of ice. As I watched that I realized that Christmas had come once again.
>
> —*The Guideposts Christmas Treasury*, [New York: Doubleday, 1972), 201.

That touching story raises a question for us to think about together: what is Christmas, and when does it come? Surely Christmas is more than a date on a calendar. Surely Christmas is more than a vague annual nod in the direction of Bethlehem. Surely Christmas is more than poinsettias and presents and parades and pageants, as nice as those are. What puts the meaning of Christmas deep into our souls? What writes the Christmas spirit indelibly on our hearts?

Well, of course, the essence of Christmas is love, God's incredible love for us, expressed when he sent his only Son into the world to save us. "Love Came Down at Christmas"— that's how the hymn writer puts it. That's the answer to our question. Whenever and wherever we receive God's sacrificial love, whenever and wherever we pass it on to others, whenever and wherever God's love is accepted and shared, Christmas comes once again!

But how does that happen? Let me bring the answer closer to home with three observations.

When We Love God, There Is Christmas

When we, like the shepherds, fall down in awe, wonder, and commitment before the manger of God's love, there is Christmas! When we, like the three wise men, give our best to the Master, there is Christmas! When we, like Mary and Joseph, trust and obey God and try our best to do God's will, there is Christmas!

A colleague and friend of mine served for many years as senior minister out west. He tells about an uncomfortable experience he had in a church he served some years ago. In that church, a man had been unusually loud and coarse and boisterous and overbearing, and on many occasions the man had embarrassed the life out of him in public. Every time he saw my friend, the man would shout, "Attention, everybody! Here comes the man of God! Look, everybody, the man of God is here!"

In crowded cafeterias, in busy hotel lobbies, in noisy sports arenas, in congested supermarkets, in quiet libraries, even in elegant restaurants, every time this man saw him he would point dramatically and shout, "Here comes the man of God!"

Now, let me hurry to say that my friend is not ashamed of being a Christian or a minister, but the way the man so blatantly pointed him out was disconcerting. He is a bit shy and reserved, and the man's booming announcement embarrassed him. He said he sort of felt like Clark Kent with his cover blown!

Then one day, after embarrassing my minister friend again, the man spoke directly to him and said, "So how is the man of God today?" "Just fine, thank you," he replied, then asked, "By the way, whose man are you?" The man was silent. He didn't know what to say. He probably didn't like the question very much. Maybe he detected a little irritation in it somewhere. But if we stop to think about it, the question is a good one: By the way, whose man are you? Whose woman are you? Whose child? Whose person? Whose disciple?

One of the best-known and most beloved verses in all the Bible is John 3:16: "For God so loved the world that he gave his only Son, so that everyone who believes in him may not perish but have eternal life" (NRSV). Listen! That's what Christmas is really all about. We needed a Savior and God sent us one. We needed a Messiah and God sent us one. We needed a Christ and God sent us one. God so loved the world that he gave the world his only Son.

When we bow down before that, when we come to grips with that, when we accept God's love, when we receive the Messiah into our hearts and commit our lives in faith to him, whenever and wherever that happens, there is Christmas. Whenever and wherever that happens, Christmas comes once again.

WHEN WE LOVE OUR FAMILIES, THERE IS CHRISTMAS

From that very first silent and holy night long ago in Bethlehem, Christmas has been a family matter. Just as the shepherds were drawn to the stable, even so at Christmas today we are drawn toward home. We feel a longing to go home for Christmas, to be with our families. Unfortunately, in many homes this Christmas there will be a chill in the air. You see, there is a big difference between everybody being at home…and being at home with everybody.

Sadly, in some families there is estrangement, alienation, division, uneasiness, tension, bitterness, and hostility, made all the more graphic by the sacredness of the Christmas season. And that is so pathetic, so sad, so tragic to me. How many squabbles will break out this Christmas because somebody in a family got mad? How many obscenities will be screamed? How many embarrassing scenes will unfold? How many people will be injured or killed because some family members can't get along this Christmas?

A few years ago, a young college student came to see me. It was just a few days after Christmas, and I could tell immediately that she was happy. Her face was radiant, glowing with joy. "We had the best Christmas ever," she told me. I answered, "Oh, you got some nice presents, did you?" "Well," she said,

"I did get some wonderful gifts, but that wasn't what made it special." She paused for a moment, then said, "Jim, I'm twenty years old now. And for the first time in my twenty years, Mom and Dad didn't get into a big fight at Christmas! It was the best Christmas we ever had!"

Whenever and wherever there is peace and harmony and tenderness and respect and thoughtfulness and caring in the family, Christmas comes once again. When we love God, and when we love our families, there is Christmas!

WHEN WE LOVE OTHER PEOPLE, THERE IS CHRISTMAS

Many years ago, there lived in a small village a cobbler by the name of Conrad. Day by day, early and late, the tap, tap, tap of his hammer could be heard as he mended the shoes brought to him by the villagers. Though alone and poor, this kindly older man always had a warm and friendly word for everyone. As a result, many folks took lighter hearts away from his hut, along with their carefully mended shoes.

Now, Christmas is a time when families draw close together, but Conrad had no family with whom he could share his Christmas. On Christmas morning, some neighbors, thinking how lonely Conrad must feel, decided to pay him a visit. They found him sweeping away the snow in front of his home, and to their surprise his face was radiant and happy as he greeted them.

As they entered his house, they gazed in amazement. Instead of a dreary room, they saw a place made festive with holly and evergreen. Christmas decorations brightened the walls and hung gracefully from the rafters. And the table was set for two. Obviously, Conrad was expecting a guest. "Who is coming to visit you?" the neighbors asked. Conrad replied, "Last night the Lord appeared to me in a dream. He told me that I would not be alone on Christmas Day, for he himself was coming to be my guest. That is why I have prepared so joyfully. Everything is ready now. I am waiting for him to come."

After the neighbors left, Conrad sat by the window, quietly watching and waiting for the Lord to come. As he watched, the minutes passed into hours, but he scarcely noticed because he was so excited. While he watched, a beggar passed his window, ragged, weary, almost frozen in the harsh winter winds. Conrad called him in. He offered the beggar the warmth of his humble home and gave him some shoes for his frozen feet.

After the beggar left, an old woman hobbled by, carrying on her back a heavy load of firewood. Conrad ran out, lifted the load from her back, and helped her into his little home. There he gave her some food for her starved body, and after she had rested a bit he helped the woman on her way.

Once again Conrad positioned himself by the window to watch for his Lord. This time he heard the sound of a child sobbing. Conrad opened his front door and found a little girl wandering lost and frightened in the snow. Some warm milk and soothing words stilled the frightened cries, and soon afterward Conrad restored the lost child to her mother's arms. Once more Conrad returned to his vigil. But now the sun was sinking, and the wintry Christmas day was coming to an end.

But where was his promised guest? Anxious and weary and somewhat disappointed, Conrad dropped to his knees and prayed, "Oh, Lord, where were you? I waited and watched for you all day. Why didn't you come?"

Out of the silence came a voice: "Oh, Conrad, my Conrad, don't be dismayed. This very day, three times I came to your door. Three times my shadow crossed your floor. I was the beggar with frozen feet. I was the woman you fed. I was a little girl who was lost."

The message of this story is a big part of Christmas: "Truly I tell you, just as you did it to one of the least of these who are members of my family, you did it to me." When we see Christ in other people and love them, then at that precise moment Christmas comes once again.

When we love God, when we love our families, when we love other people, there is Christmas. The Christmas gift of love is surely a Christmas gift that won't break!

DISCUSSION QUESTIONS

1. Describe a time when you experienced the gift of love. How did it make you feel? How did you respond?

2. What connections do you see between John 3:16 and the Christmas season?

3. List some of the many ways that love of family can be shown. What are some examples from your own experience?

4. What are some ways in which the act of loving other people brings about and enhances Christmas?

5. Why is love the perfect gift? List some of the many reasons this gift is cherished.

6. What are some ways we can show our love for God at Christmas?

PRAYER

Dear God, thank you for the gift of love. May we share this gift with others and learn how to love unconditionally. Help us during this Christmas season to practice love in action with family, friends, and strangers. Amen.

FOCUS FOR THE WEEK

This week, consider ways to express your love of other people. Take some risks in doing so with family and friends. Practice acts of love and kindness toward strangers. Respond to others as Jesus would do, in compassion and with a willingness to meet human needs.

Devotions

CHAPTER TWO

LOVE CASTS OUT FEAR

Luke 2:10-20

Tonkeybell came to live with our family on a cool fall night when our middle daughter, Lydia, came into the house from playing and we found her hair matted with blood. Upon closer inspection, we found that Lydia had a large cut on the top of her head. She hadn't noticed! We still don't know how it happened, but we knew immediately it needed attention. We took her to the emergency room. Upon our arrival, the first thing the nurse did was give a scared three-year-old and two scared parents a soft, stuffed bear. It had been made and donated by a ladies' group at a local church. They had a big box of them to give to young children who came to the ER.

The nurse asked Lydia what she wanted to name him and she responded immediately, "Tonkeybell!" We think now it may have been an attempt to say "Tinkerbell," but whatever Lydia's original intent, she named him Tonkeybell. And lo all these years he has remained Tonkeybell.

Tonkeybell is a part of our family. He goes everywhere with Lydia. He accompanies her to bed of course, but he also goes on road trips, airplane trips, and walks in the neighborhood. Wherever we go, Tonkeybell goes. On more than one occasion, we have been a couple miles down the road only to discover that Tonkeybell is not with us. We turn around and go home.

As I'm sure you have picked up on, Tonkeybell is Lydia's equivalent of a security blanket, blankey, teddy bear, or whatever it may have been for you. Psychologists call it a *"comfort object"*: an item that is used to provide psychological comfort to someone facing fear. It is common for a child to attach to something especially when they go through a difficult time, a transition, or a hospital visit.

The most famous comfort object bearer is, of course, Linus Van Pelt. If you don't recognize the name, I am referring to Charlie Brown's best friend Linus from the Charles Schulz *Peanuts* cartoons. Linus is known for carrying his little blue blanket everywhere he goes. You will be hard pressed to find Linus without his blue blankey, and he usually has his thumb in his mouth as well. When you see Linus, you see the blanket. It gives him comfort. He is a nervous little dude and the old worn-out blanket, like my daughter's Tonkeybell, is familiar and soft and pushes his fears away for a bit.

Recently, there was a sort of discovery that made its way through the blogosphere around Christmastime. Around the time that the popular *Charlie Brown Christmas* TV special was celebrating its fiftieth anniversary, there was much written about a newly noticed, almost hidden moment toward the end of the show. You may remember the end of the show when a down-in-the-dumps Charlie Brown wonders what Christmas is all about. The climactic scene features fearful, anxious Linus becoming the almost hero of the cartoon when he takes one minute to recite Scripture from his heart. The scene is still blasted across national TV every year. The discovery that gained attention is something in this scene I had never noticed before. During the speech, as Linus recites the Christmas story from Luke 2, he drops his blanket when he comes to the part about the shepherds receiving the news of Jesus' birth, when he quotes the angels saying, "Fear not."

Fear not.

At the words "Fear not," Linus throws his blanket down and finishes the story with both hands free to give gesture to the amazing announcement of the gift of love in the baby Jesus. There are many messages of Christmas, but there is one that everybody in the story received and receives. And it is, "Fear not." Do not be afraid. It seems that everybody needed to hear it.

Zechariah and Elizabeth, an old couple who were ushered into the story at retirement age and found themselves having a baby, heard it. "Fear not," the angel told Zechariah in the temple (Luke 1:13 KJV).

51

Mary is greeted as the unsuspecting teenage mom of the Son of God. Nothing scary about that right? She got a big "Fear not" from the angel as well (Luke 1:30 KJV).

Joseph got his word in a dream. "Fear not" Joseph, take Mary home as your wife (Matthew 1:20 KJV).

And then the shepherds, as Linus recounted, out working in the fields at night, heard, "Fear not: for, behold, I bring you good tidings of great joy, which shall be to all people" (Luke 2:10 KJV).

Advent, which literally means "arrival," is about the arrival of a gift of love so powerful that it casts out fear. It causes us to throw our comfort objects down. As someone who has struggled with anxiety in my life, I have always related most to Linus in the Charlie Brown cartoons. Well, him and Pig-Pen. But I know what it's like to hold on to some things so tightly when it seems like everything else is scary. I know the feeling of fists clinched when facing the uncertain, sometimes when facing just normal days.

What is your comfort object? What are you holding on to so tightly that it gives you a sense of security in a scary world? What are you afraid of right now? What do you fear regarding your kids...regarding your job...regarding your health...regarding our world? What are you afraid of?

Advent is a time when we set our fears down and believe that God's love holds something for us that could change everything. What would it mean for you to drop everything like Linus and the shepherds, to rush fearlessly down the hill to where the baby is?

The gift of love casts out fear. In 1 John 4:18 we read that "there is no fear in love, but perfect love drives out fear." In the arrival of the Christ Child, we encounter perfect love. The gift of this love pushes fear away. Just like my love as a father for Lydia on the night her scalp was stitched up held a deep desire for her to be comforted and at peace, God's love for us comes to our injured place with a love that brings comfort and peace.

The gift of love comes to where we are. We see in the story of Jesus' birth that God comes to where we are. Mary and Joseph are not transported out of their crazy world or even out of their earthly obligations. Instead God comes right to where they are in a stable in the middle of the census. Likewise, God shows up to the shepherds, third-shift workers, right there in the field in the middle of the night. The very nature of love is that it comes to where we are. Jesus comes to us.

The gift of love means that we aren't alone. When Zechariah went into the temple, he was the only priest that was allowed to go. One of the reasons he was scared to death when an angel starting talking to him (as if that alone isn't scary enough) is because he thought no one else was there. But Zechariah wasn't alone. The angel told Zechariah, "Don't be afraid," and then "your prayers have been heard" (Luke 1:13). God had heard the prayer of Zechariah's heart. God heard his prayer for the people of Israel who were longing for a Messiah, and it seems implied that God had heard Zechariah's prayer for a child. Zechariah actually hadn't been alone when he prayed. Zechariah hadn't been alone in his disappointment. He hadn't been alone when he had shaken his fist at God wondering if God was listening. In the same way, God's love for us means God has heard the longing and aching of our hearts.

The gift of love leads us to long for more. The gift of love causes our hearts to awaken. As fear is pushed away, we let go of our comfort objects and use our hands to express the power of the story as we communicate it to others. Without tightly clinched fists, we begin to dream of what is to come. Without the companion of fear, we begin to wonder what life will look like with the new reality of world-changing love in our very presence.

It leads me to ask you a risky question, but I'm going for it. Look deep inside your heart, a heart that may have given up on this question, a heart that may be clouded with fear and anxiety. Still, I ask you . . .

What are you longing for?

God's gift of love gives us permission to ask the question. Is it for a relationship to be restored? Is it for a bill to be paid? Is it for forgiveness? Is your longing for someone else, for a child, for a parent? Maybe it is for something bigger than yourself. Do you long for peace in places where there is war? Do you long for racial equality or for refugees to be welcomed?

The promise of Jesus' arrival in the world is that, yes, Jesus has come to us, but also that God hears our longings! The shepherds' hearts in the middle of the night longed for what only God could bring, and God brought it to them and invited them to see Jesus.

Yes, it's not the way we expected. It's never the way we expected, but it's good. Saying that it is unexpected doesn't mean we have a sneaky God who plays tricks on us. It means we trust in a God who knows and hears our deepest longings even better than we do, and longs to come to us.

That's right. We have a longing, but God, too, has a longing. Long before we ever ached for God, or ached for healing, or ached for forgiveness, God ached and longed for us. It is common for us as we consider God's desire to come into our world to quickly begin to find reasons to disqualify ourselves from the things God wants to do. It is for them, we think, but surely not for us. But the Advent Scriptures say not so fast. It is for the old and the young. It is for those who are faithful and those who struggle with faith. It is for kings and common shepherds. So if you have been quick to disqualify yourself from the list of those to whom God wants to come, the Christmas story gives you no precedent for that. God's fear-busting love is for everyone.

At the end of Linus's speech about the true meaning of Christmas, he picks his blanket back up. He picks up the blanket and walks over to Charlie Brown, and they walk outside to a pathetic, scrawny Christmas tree. It is at that moment as they stand before what seems an unworthy tree that Linus steps forward again, takes the blanket—the symbol of his fears—and wraps it around the base of the tree. The blanket turns the frail tree into a beautiful, majestic Christmas tree.

Tonkeybell is an old bear now. He is worn out. You can't make out the features of his face anymore. They have been loved away. We are not, though, giving up on Tonkeybell. We

55

have no plans to trade him in for a newer model. It's interesting, when we look at Tonkeybell now, we rarely think of the scary night when he came into our life. Instead, his presence is a joy as we remember all the things we have been through together.

Most often the symbol of our weakness and fear is not something we discard. The reminder of our fear becomes something different because of our belief that God's love casts out fear. That thing that was a symbol of weakness becomes a symbol of power.

That's the Jesus story.

A cross, a symbol of death, becomes the symbol of life.

Broken bread and poured-out juice become for us a sign of wholeness and forgiveness.

A baby wrapped in a blanket in a feeding trough becomes our new king.

And it's for you. He's for you. The good news is for *all* the people. He is the Messiah, the Lord. This will be a sign to you: you will find a baby wrapped in a blanket and lying in a manger.

Day 1

Do you remember your comfort object as a kid, or those of your kids or others in your family? What leads to a child letting go of the object as he or she ages? As you take some quiet moments today to consider the story of Jesus' arrival into the world, consider those things that you still hold on to that give you comfort. What is your comfort object today? What are you holding on to? What would it look like for you to let go of these things, if only for a moment, to place your trust in God more deeply?

Day 2

The word *Advent* means "arrival" or "coming." Jesus' arrival in the world was a gift of love that allows us to move past some of the fears in our lives. Is there something that you are waiting on, something that you need to arrive in order for you to put down your fear? How does your understanding of Jesus' coming into the world inform how you think about what you need to happen in your life?

Day 3

We can see some of the things that the characters in the Advent stories were longing for. Zechariah and Elizabeth were longing for a child. Joseph was longing to protect Mary. What are you longing for? If the gift of love leads us to long for more, what would the *more* be for you?

Day 4

It is easy to think that we aren't the ones for whom Jesus would now come. We are too old, too young, we've made too many mistakes, or we've missed our chance. Yet we see in the Bible that there is no such criteria for disqualification to encounter God. The good news is for all people. What insecurities do you have that hold you back from encountering and being used by God? Do you believe that the good news is for you, too?

Day 5

We all have things in our lives that remind us of our weaknesses and fears. What symbols of your weakness or fear do you see in your life? How could these become symbols of the overcoming power of God?

Day 6

The angels announced to the shepherds, "Don't be afraid! Look! I bring good news to you—wonderful, joyous news for all people." What does the good news being for all the people mean to you? Who can you take good news to today?

Day 7

As we close this week, where we have marveled over God's gift of love to us through Jesus, think of an intentional way that you can share love. Look for an opportunity where you can share love with those who may consider themselves unlovable. In doing so, you will be a part of the story of Christ's coming.

Chapter Three

THE GIFT OF JOY

3

THE GIFT OF JOY

Now all of this took place so that what the Lord had spoken through the prophet would be fulfilled:

> Look! A virgin will become pregnant
> and give birth to a son,
>   And they will call him, *Emmanuel*.

(Emmanuel *means "God with us."*)

When Joseph woke up, he did just as an angel from God commanded and took Mary as his wife. But he didn't have sexual relations with her until she gave birth to a son. Joseph called him Jesus.

Matthew 1:22-25

A young mother wanted her two preschool-aged children to learn the real meaning of Christmas, so early that December she brought home a small manger scene. The figurines in the manger scene were made of wood, so they were pretty much indestructible—and easy for little hands to pick up and move around.

The children loved the manger scene, and they loved being able to arrange and rearrange the figurines in creative and childlike ways. As you might imagine, sometimes the figurines would disappear and later show up in the most fascinating places around the house.

Interestingly, the character that most often disappeared was Jesus. The mother would walk by and see that Jesus was missing again. Once she found him on the windowsill in her daughter's room. How appropriate, thought the mother: Jesus was born in a stable, but he moved out of the manger to go with us and watch over us wherever we may go.

A few days before Christmas, the Jesus figurine disappeared again. The mother looked all over the house and could not find him anywhere. When time came to put the manger scene away, Jesus was still missing. She called the children to the manger scene and asked, "Where is Jesus?" Her five-year-old daughter scrunched up her shoulder and stuck out her hands, palms upward, in that universal gesture that means "Search me. I don't know. I have no idea. I don't have a clue."

The mother then turned to her two-year-old son and asked, "Do you know where Jesus is?" Her son became very animated and began talking a mile a minute. But, as is sometimes the case with two-year-olds, it sounded like gibberish. The boy knew what he was saying, but his mother and sister couldn't understand it.

Finally the boy went over, took his mother by the hand, and led her to his room. He pointed to his bed. The mother pulled back the covers and looked, with no luck. Then the boy pointed to his pillow. Finally, she found the Jesus figurine—under her son's pillow!

Isn't that beautiful? You see, for many two-year-olds, bedtime is scary time. It's dark in the room, and they feel all alone. But this young boy felt safe and secure because Jesus was there with him!

That's the good news of Christmas, isn't it? We find that incredible truth expressed with these magnificent words in the first chapter of Matthew: "His name shall be called Emmanuel, which means, 'God is with us.'"

Here is the great truth of Christmas, the great message of Christmas, the great promise of Christmas, the great joy of Christmas, all wrapped up in that one word, *Emmanuel*, which means God is always with us!

The good news of Christmas gives us a deep sense of hope, of love, and of joy. Let me tell you what I mean.

THE JOY OF ENCOURAGEMENT

In this world, people get criticized too much, "put down" too much, and "fussed at" too much, so we in the church (who are the children of Christmas) need to be the sons and daughters of encouragement. The message of Christmas is good news, glad tidings, great joy. Christ came to lift people up, not tear them down. Christ came to save people, not destroy them. We would do well to pick up his torch and take on his spirit of joyful encouragement.

Have you heard about the little boy who was in the school Christmas play? He was playing the part of an angel. He was to come to the shepherds in the field and announce Christ's birth with enthusiasm and excitement. But he was having real trouble learning his part. He was especially finding it difficult to say his line, "Behold, I bring you glad tidings of great joy." The boy didn't normally talk that way, so he found the line hard to memorize. The drama teacher worked with him and explained that "glad tidings" simply meant good news. Finally, the boy learned his part. But on the night of the play, the boy got stage fright and forgot his line. Instead of saying, "Behold, I bring you glad tidings of great joy," the little angel made this Christmas play different from any other by suddenly running all over the stage, flapping his wings wildly, and shouting over and over, "Boy, have I got good news for you!"

That's part of our task as Christians, isn't it? We need to say to a scared, anxious, confused, fretful world, "Boy, have we got good news for you!" The good news is that we can make it because God is with us and will see us through. Our part of that good news is saying to people near us, "I care about you," "I believe in you," "I trust you," "You can do it."

Maybe the best gift we can give someone we love this Christmas is a gift that will not break: the joy of encouragement.

THE JOY OF THOUGHTFULNESS

One of the things I love most about Christmas is the way it brings out people's thoughtfulness. Christmas cards, gifts, flowers, food, phone calls, e-mails—these wonderful gestures of thoughtfulness are woven deeply into the fabric of Christmas.

Some years ago, when I was on the staff of the First United Methodist Church in Shreveport, Louisiana, some members of our outreach committee came to me a few days before Christmas with a concern and a plan. They were concerned that some people in our community might be hungry or lonely on Christmas Day. Their plan was to open our church fellowship hall on Christmas afternoon and offer free food and warm fellowship—a Christmas party—to anyone who might be hungry or lonely. I asked them if they would be willing to give up their Christmas afternoon to work in the kitchen. They said they would be glad to and that they had already recruited several others to help. So we announced to the city that anyone who might be hungry or lonely on Christmas afternoon could come to the church between noon and five o'clock to enjoy Christmas carols, fellowship, and a complimentary meal.

Just after lunch on Christmas afternoon, I drove to the church to see how things were going. It was about two o'clock when I got there. As I went inside, I met several members of our outreach committee coming out the door and heading for home. "What happened?" I asked. "Is it over? Didn't anybody show up?" A committee member answered, "Oh, they are in there for sure. About three hundred are eating right now. The only reason we are leaving is that some new workers came in to relieve us." I asked, "Who?" The committee member smiled and said, "Why don't you go into the kitchen and see for yourself."

When I went into the kitchen, I was moved to tears by what I saw: There was my good friend, a rabbi, along with fourteen members of his temple, who had told our people, "This is your special day. Go home and be with your families, and we will work for you."

Isn't that something? One of the most moving Christmas gifts I ever saw came from a group of Jewish friends who had heard what we were trying to do and had responded with joy—the joy of thoughtfulness.

THE JOY OF GRACIOUSNESS

The joy of gracious, sacrificial love—that's what it's all about, isn't it?

Glenn Kittler writes of a Franciscan priest named Father Bonaventure, who gave a Christmas party for some Native American children of the Papago tribe near Tucson, Arizona. It was their first Christmas party. There were games and races, with prizes for the winners. One little boy named Luis Pablo was especially excited to be there. He told Father Bonaventure that he needed to win three prizes. Luis tried hard. He entered every game and ran in every race but, much to his dismay, did not win a single prize. At the end of the party, the children formed a line, and to each of them Father Bonaventure presented a bag of hard candy. When eight-year-old Luis Pablo received his, he asked for three more. Father Bonaventure refused him sternly.

However, Luis explained he only wanted empty bags, so Father Bonaventure shrugged and thought, "Why not?" He gave Luis three bags, and the boy left, smiling. Later, the priest looked out the window and saw Luis sitting with the three bags open beside him, carefully dividing his candy into the bags. Father Bonaventure suddenly remembered that Luis had two little brothers and a sister at home who were too young to come to the party. Going into the party room, Father Bonaventure collected all the remaining candy into a large bag, went outside, and gave it to Luis.

"Here's your prize," he said.

"Prize?" Luis asked, suspicious. "What for?"

"All during the party I was watching to see which one of you had the true spirit of Christmas . . . you win."

—*The Guideposts Christmas Treasury*,
(New York: Doubleday, 1972), 206

The essence of Christmas is the joy of gracious, sacrificial love. Christ came to show us what God is like and what God wants us to be like, and the word is *love*: love came down at Christmas, and the joy it brings is the best and most unbreakable gift of all!

DISCUSSION QUESTIONS

1. Name some times in life when we experience joy. What are some examples from your own life?

2. The name *Emmanuel* means "God is with us." What are some reasons that this is so?

3. What does "joyful encouragement" mean to you? What are some examples from your own life?

4. In your experience, does Christmas bring out thoughtfulness in people? Why do you think this is?

5. What are some ways in which we experience the joy of graciousness at Christmas?

6. When you think of the Christmas gift of joy, what thoughts or images come to mind?

PRAYER

Dear God, thank you for the gift of joy and for the way it brightens our days. Help us give joy to others through what we say and do. Show us how to make this Christmas a true season of joy. Amen.

FOCUS FOR THE WEEK

Practice being a joyful person this week. Give joy to others. Look for opportunities to open the eyes of others to the joys of the season. Count your blessings and the many joys of your life.

$\mathcal{D}$evotions
CHAPTER THREE

THE JOY OF GOD WITH US

Matthew 1:22-25

"What if the place you go for solace and security is in flames?"

One Tuesday morning during Advent in 2016, I awoke with this question on my heart and mind. I had gone to bed watching the news reports about our beloved Great Smoky Mountains burning. A forest fire raged out of control taking homes, businesses, and, most tragically, lives. As a lifelong Tennessean, those woods represent for me much more than a pretty place to go see leaves in the fall. For me and many in our area, the forests in the mountains of eastern Tennessee are a part of our childhood. Those woods are where my dad taught me to fish, where my mom taught me how to be quiet and listen on a hike, and where my brother and I have spent many a night staring at the stars and talking about our lives. "What if the place you go for solace and security is in flames?" I wondered. What if your getaway is taken away? That Tuesday I felt an odd feeling. What will it feel like to walk the trails that for so long held life and hope, and now see ash and destruction?

Some of us know all too well how that feels. A spouse who was your safe and secure place has been taken away through divorce, betrayal, or death. A business venture that wasn't just a job, but your dream, for one reason or another is now up in flames. Some of us know how an illness or a layoff or a loss can take away so much. Some of us know how depression or anxiety can be like a smoke-filled cloud covering what once was a beautiful view. What do we do when tragedy strikes? What do we do when we lose something we love? What do we do when our lives simply don't go the way we thought they would? Can there still be joy?

Yes, God says. There can be joy. That's what Advent is all about. It's about our hoping, believing, waiting for God to come and make something out of our mess. We wait for God to step into what appears to be impending doom and save us. Advent holds out the belief that in the midst of that kind of waiting, God brings the gift of joy.

Each year I look forward to singing one of my favorite Christmas carols, "O Holy Night." I like the song because it acknowledges that Advent is a time during which we sing about *light* because we are in *darkness*. We sing about *hope* because we are *longing* for something more. We sing about *joy* because our hearts know *sadness*.

72

Long lay the world in sin and error pining,
Till He appeared and the soul felt its worth.
A thrill of hope—the weary world rejoices,
For yonder breaks a new and glorious morn!
Fall on your knees!

Our world is weary (maybe you are weary), but joy is coming.

There is a strange story in the Book of Isaiah. It's about King Ahaz. Ahaz was the ruler of Judah, who reigned in Jerusalem. Ahaz wasn't a good king. He was one of the worst, actually. Ahaz was, though, God's anointed one for a period of time, and Isaiah 7 depicts a crazy conversation between God and an insecure, impulsive king.

Ahaz has learned that two other kings are conspiring to come and take him and Jerusalem out. Jerusalem, the city of God, is the place of solace and security for the people of God. It is the place where God's people travel during the year to come close to God. These two kings want to dethrone Ahaz and put a new king in his place, because he has refused to join an alliance with them. And they march against Jerusalem, the place of solace and security for Ahaz and the people of Judah. The two other kings attack the city, but they cannot get past the walls. It is a close call.

"The hearts of Ahaz and his people were shaken, as the trees of the forest are shaken by the wind" (Isaiah 7:2 NIV).

The two kings have come to invade Jerusalem and tear the throne away from Ahaz, and Ahaz is naturally afraid. He is shaking like a tree in a storm. But, remember Isaiah 7 is about a conversation between God and the king. God tells Ahaz, as we say in Tennessee, "It ain't going to happen!"

> *"'Let us invade Judah; let us tear it apart and divide*
> *it among ourselves, and make the son of Tabeel king*
> *over it.' Yet this is what the Sovereign Lord says:*
>
> *'It will not take place,*
> *it will not happen'"*
>
> (Isaiah 7:6-7 NIV)

God is so sure of this that God tells Ahaz to ask for a sign that it will be so. In a strange response, Ahaz tells God, "I won't ask; I won't test the LORD" (Isaiah 7:12). God says, in essence, that God will give Ahaz a sign anyway. And in one of the most famous Old Testament Scriptures of prophecy, we read in Isaiah 7:14 (NIV): "Therefore the Lord himself will give you a sign: The virgin will conceive and give birth to a son, and will call him Immanuel."

Immanuel means "God with us."

The people of God are afraid. Their king is shaking in his boots. They feel as if they will lose their place of solace and security. To them God says, "I am here. I am going to give you a sign that I'm here, and the sign will be..." Wait for it. "The sign will be a baby born from a virgin named God is with us." This almost puts a smile on your face, right? "A virgin will conceive" is pretty much the definition of impossible. What could be more impossible?

God often uses the most impossible thing you can think of as the very sign that God is with us. And in the impossible being made possible, we find joy.

God, in a time when it seems we will lose our place of security, gives a sign. God gives a sign to say it won't happen.

The reason that Isaiah 7:14 is famous is because of something that happens in another story some seven hundred years later. This story is about Mary. Mary becomes probably the most famous woman of all time, but in Luke 1 all we know is that she is a virgin who is planning to get married. In this story, God has another conversation, this time not with a king, but with a young woman who is betrothed but not yet married.

As a pastor who has worked a great deal with young adults, I get the honor of officiating many weddings. I don't know how much time you have spent around young women who are planning to get married, but they tend to be quite focused. Every other week or so I will meet with a young woman and a young man who are planning to get married. If there is anything consistent in my experience, it is that the young woman usually has a focused vision for their wedding. These women are generally quite pleasant, but you can tell they have painted this dream in their minds and hearts for some time, and they are now laser focused on what is coming.

I don't know if Mary had any similarities to the young women I get a chance to meet, but it is reasonable to think Mary had some expectation about how her life would go in the future. Maybe she hadn't planned it down to the last detail of the wedding day, but surely she had a vision for how that day and her years with Joseph would unfold. All of that was taken away in one simple message from God. "You will conceive and give birth to a son," she is told (Luke 1:31). Those of you who have learned that message—that you are pregnant—through a doctor or a test, regardless of circumstances, know that statement changes everything. It changes everything for Mary.

Whatever she was planning will never happen now. Mary, who becomes the picture of faithfulness and obedience moving forward, offers one pounding, cosmic question to God.

"How?"

"How will this happen since I haven't had sexual relations with a man?" (Luke 1:34).

What is Mary saying? She's saying that this is impossible. I wonder though if the question brought a smile to her face. I wonder if the hope that began to build in her heart brought her joy.

God often uses the most impossible thing you can think of as the very sign that God is with you. And in the impossible being made possible we find joy.

The Jesus story teaches us that we can find joy even in scary and impossible situations.

Ahaz, the king of Judah, is literally shaking like a tree in the wind. Here he is told, "Be careful and stay calm. Don't fear, and don't lose heart over these two pieces of smoking torches" (Isaiah 7:4). God speaks words of courage in scary times that lead us to joy.

Mary is told, "Don't be afraid, Mary. God is honoring you" (Luke 1:30). God speaks words of courage in scary times that lead us to joy.

It is why at Christmastime we often find ourselves the most generous. We give and serve those who are vulnerable and find themselves in scary places because the Jesus story leads us to want to share this joy and hope with others. We want to lead others to ask the question, "How can this be?" We hope they will wonder how God could do the impossible. The answer to "How can this be?" is "God is with us."

Knowing God is with us is the gift that brings joy.

Remember the sign of Immanuel (God with us) is a baby being born to a woman who has no business having a baby. Right now, for some of us we are experiencing a fire that seems to be burning out of control. It may look like your life is going up in flames. Or like Ahaz, we feel that there is no way to hold off impending doom. Or perhaps like Mary we find ourselves in a situation that seems impossible. I had this plan! I thought my life would go this way, and now in one night it is gone. How? How can this be?

The story of Jesus' birth tells us that hope is coming, and with the hope of Jesus comes a gift we surely did not see coming. It's the gift of joy. What's our sign? A baby born in a manger.

The same Tuesday morning that I turned on the news to see about the destruction of the Smoky Mountains, I received a text from my mother-in-law. It said, "Leah is here!"

It doesn't mean a lot to you, I know, but it meant something to my family. We had been waiting for Leah for nine months. We had been praying for her before she had a name. She was my first niece. Right there on my phone, I saw "Leah is here!" and my heart soared. I teared up with love for a baby I had never met, but I had been waiting for.

I paused for a moment in the grief I had been feeling for a destroyed land and the loss of life. I gave thanks for Leah and for some reason wondered what her name means. I knew Leah to be a biblical name, but never thought to learn its meaning. With a quick Google search I learned that Leah means "weary." Leah means "tired."

As we have already discovered, people who understand biblical names don't worry if a name at first holds a negative meaning. Leah is in a long line of people like Mary whose names initially held a negative meaning. Yet God can take our names and change what they mean. Our Advent baby is named "weary." A baby born into a weary world. But we sit around and stare at Leah and our hearts burst with...joy. She's a sign to us. She's a gift of joy.

Followers of Jesus have our sign. If we feel we've lost what has meant safety or security or even life, we have our sign. If you have been looking for a sign, look no further. The sign for us is a baby conceived in a virgin. Crazy. Impossible. His name is Immanuel. God with us.

Day 1

Have you ever had something in your life taken away from you that once represented solace and safety? How do you experience that loss today? As we remember that Advent is for those who experience loss and are still waiting for God, ask God to come and meet you in your place of loss. Invite God to be with you not just in the places where you feel strong, but in the places where you experience brokenness.

Day 2

In the song "O Holy Night," we sing that a thrill of hope causes the weary world to rejoice. Do you feel tired today? What makes you weary? How can you find joy in your weariness?

Day 3

Why do you think God used the sign of a baby born of a virgin to show us that God is with us? How has God used the seemingly impossible to show you God's presence and give you joy?

Day 4

Immanuel means "God with us." Today you will encounter those who do not know God's presence. Today you might talk with someone who feels that God has left him or her. What sign can you give today to show God's presence to those who desperately need to know Immanuel?

Day 5

Over and over in the Advent stories God says, "Do not be afraid." What helps you to feel "not afraid" in scary times? How do you experience God saying to you "Do not be afraid"?

Day 6

What brings you joy? Do something today that gives you joy and causes you to rejoice.

Day 7

As we close this week where we have marveled over God's gift of joy to us through Jesus, think of an intentional way that you can share joy. Look for an opportunity where you can share joy with those who may find themselves in despair. In doing so, you will be a part of the story of Christ's coming.

Chapter Four

THE GIFT OF PEACE

4

THE GIFT OF PEACE

Nearby shepherds were living in the fields, guarding their sheep at night. The Lord's angel stood before them, the Lord's glory shone around them, and they were terrified.

The angel said, "Don't be afraid! Look! I bring good news to you—wonderful, joyous news for all people. Your savior is born today in David's city. He is Christ the Lord. This is a sign for you: you will find a newborn baby wrapped snugly and lying in a manger." Suddenly a great assembly of the heavenly forces was with the angel praising God. They said, "Glory to God in heaven, and on earth peace among those whom he favors."

Luke 2:8-14

A beautiful old Christmas legend tells of how God called the angels of heaven together one day for a special choir rehearsal. God told them of a special song they were to learn, a song they would sing at a very significant occasion. So the angels went to work on it. They rehearsed long and hard, with great focus and intensity. In fact, some of the angels grumbled a bit, but God insisted on a very high standard for the choir.

As time passed, the choir improved in tone, in rhythm, and in quality. Finally, God announced that they were ready, but then God shocked them a bit. God told them that they would sing the song only once, and only on one night. There would be just one performance. Again, some of the angels grumbled. The song was so extraordinarily beautiful, and they had it down pat now. Surely they could sing it many times. God just smiled and told them that when the time came, they would understand.

Finally one night, God called the choir together. The angels gathered above a field just outside of Bethlehem. "It's time," God told them, and the angels sang their song. Oh, my, did they sing it! "Glory to God in heaven, and on earth peace among those whom he favors." And as the angels sang, they knew there would never be another night like this one and that there would never be another birth like this birth in Bethlehem.

When the angels returned to heaven, God reminded them that they could hum the song occasionally as individuals if they wanted to, but they would not sing it again formally as an angelic choir. One angel was bold enough to step forward and ask God why not. They had performed it so beautifully. It had felt so right. Why couldn't they sing that great song anymore?

God smiled. "Because," God said, "my son has been born, and now earth must do the singing!"

Once each year, Christmas comes around again to remind us of what God said: that God's Son has come to earth, and now we must do the singing! And look at how we have tried. Without question, one of the best and most beloved parts of the Christmas celebration is the music. The good news of Christmas is so awesome, so full of wonder, that it's not enough just to talk about it. We have to burst forth in song. We have to sing it.

Think of it! There are the traditional anthems of Handel, Beethoven, Mozart, and Bach, as well as the powerful modern works of Rutter, Davis, and Landes. There are beloved carols such as "O Little Town of Bethlehem," "Joy to the World," "The First Noel," "Silent Night," and "O Come, All Ye Faithful." And there are popular songs such as "Jingle Bells," "Winter Wonderland," and "I'll Be Home for Christmas."

Once I was in a department store doing some Christmas shopping. Christmas music was playing, and I was getting into the spirit of it all, when suddenly I realized that I was singing along with Vince Gill. Vince and I were performing the hymn "Let There Be Peace on Earth and Let It Begin with Me." Vince and I were sounding pretty good, mainly because Vince can sing and because it is a great Christmas hymn (as well as a great hymn for all seasons), with a beautiful melody and an even more beautiful life-lesson in it.

The words of that hymn are a big part of the Christmas message: God loves us and claims us as beloved children, and God wants us to live in the spirit of peaceful unity and harmony as sisters and brothers in God's family. In fact, God wants us to live each day in the spirit of peacemakers. Look at those words again: "Let there be peace on earth and let it begin with me." Let it start with me. Let me live every day as a peacemaker—in other words, in the gracious spirit of Jesus Christ.

That's the way it works. Christmas is the dramatic reminder that Christ came into this world to redeem us and to bring peace to our troubled souls. Christmas has a great gift for us, if we will only accept it in faith: the gift of peace. Christmas offers us peace with God, peace with ourselves, and peace with others.

PEACE WITH GOD

Jesus Christ came into this world to set us right with God. Jesus Christ came into the world to save us and to bring us back to God. It's what Christmas is all about.

You may have heard the old story about the elderly couple driving down the street one day. It was Christmastime, and the husband was driving. As they listened to the beautiful music of Christmas on the radio, the wife became nostalgic and said, "Herbert, do you remember how we used to sit so close together as we drove along? It was so wonderful back then. What happened?" Herbert replied, "I don't know about that. All I know is that I haven't moved."

Well, Christmas comes each year to remind us that God is not the one who has moved away from us. No! We are the ones who have moved. We are the ones who have drifted away from him.

Some years ago, a friend told me a story about taking his five-year-old son Christmas shopping one Saturday morning. It was just a day or so before Christmas, and the department store was packed with shoppers. He told his son to stay near him and not wander off, because he could get lost in the crowd. After they had shopped together for a while, he was buying something for his wife at one of the counters. When he completed the purchase, he looked back and his son was not there. He frantically searched for his son. He called out to him and rushed through the crowd looking for him, with no success. He checked the candy counter and then the toy department. Surely his son would be there! But no, his son wasn't anywhere to be found.

Just as he was starting to panic, there was an announcement over the loudspeaker: "We have a lost boy here! If you have lost your little boy, please come to the service desk." He anxiously made his way to the desk, and sure enough, there was his lost child. It was a big reunion, with lots of hugs and words of love and more visits to the candy counter and the toy department. They had been apart, but they had found each other again! They had been brought back together.

Now, think about this. The two of them had been separated because the little boy had wandered off, and it was the person who spoke over the loudspeaker who got them back together again. That person served, in a sense, as a reconciler between a father and his little boy.

In the same sense, Christ came to this earth to help us get back together with God who made us and who loves us. That's what the word *Emmanuel* means in our text: God is with us. God comes in the Christ Child to seek and save the lost. That's what Christmas is all about. That's the way we can have the peace of Christmas: to let the Christ of Christmas bring us back to the Father who loves us.

PEACE WITH OURSELVES

More and more psychologists are telling us that we can't feel good about life and other people until we feel good about ourselves. They call it a healthy self-esteem, which is simply another way of saying that we need to be right with ourselves.

Have you heard about the man who wrote a letter to the Internal Revenue Service? The letter said, "Dear sirs: I underpaid my tax bill for last year. I can't sleep at night and my conscience is bothering me. Enclosed please find $600." He then added a P.S.: "If I still can't sleep, I'll send the rest."

I once saw a fascinating movie about the famous golfer Bobby Jones. Called *Stroke of Genius*, the movie takes us back to a time when Jones was the talk of the golfing world. Bobby Jones was born on March 17, 1902, in Atlanta, Georgia. He was a child prodigy in golf, winning his first tournament at the age of six. By the time he was twelve, he was the Georgia state golf champion, and in 1921, at age nineteen, he became the youngest member of the US Walker Cup team when it journeyed to England. Between 1923 and 1930, Jones won five US amateur titles, four US Opens, three British Opens, and one British amateur title. In 1930 he achieved the "Grand Slam," winning all four of the major golf tournaments in a single calendar year, the only golfer in history ever to accomplish that feat. Amazingly, Jones retired from golf at the young age of twenty-eight. He became a lawyer, and in 1934 he helped design the Augusta National Golf Club, where he founded the noted Masters Golf Tournament.

But with all his incredible accomplishments as a golf champion, Bobby Jones may be even more well-known and respected for a tournament he didn't win! It was the US Open, and *Stroke of Genius* depicts the scene powerfully. Jones hits his ball into the rough. As he stands over the ball for his second shot, his ball moves slightly. No one else sees this, but Jones immediately tells an official that he caused his ball to move. The officials huddle up and discuss the situation. Then they come back to Jones and tell him, "Bobby, we've talked to your opponent, to all the officials, and to several people in the gallery, and nobody saw your ball move. It's your call. Are you sure you caused that ball to move?" Jones answers, "I know I did." The lead official looks at him and says, "Son, you are to be congratulated!" To which Jones says, "Sir, that is like congratulating me for not robbing a bank. I don't know how else to play the game." It was a two-stroke penalty, and (can you believe it?) Bobby Jones lost that US Open tournament by one stroke!

What he did that day prompted noted sportswriter O. B. Keeler to write these words: "Bobby Jones lost the US Open today by one stroke. In calling a penalty on himself, he demonstrated for all of us the highest ideals of sportsmanship and personal honor. I am prouder of him than if he had won." Bobby Jones said of his actions, "There are things finer than winning championships." Today, appropriately, the United States Golf Association's sportsmanship prize is named the Bobby Jones Award.

Let me ask you something. Do you feel good about your life right now? About who you are and what you've done? No matter how we feel, we can find peace with ourselves by welcoming the Prince of Peace into our hearts and lives. The only way we can be right with ourselves is to be made right by him.

PEACE WITH OTHERS

A friend of mine, in her eighties and full of life, has a very special Christmas headband. It has mistletoe above it on a spring. When she wears it, she is under the mistletoe no matter where she goes! Two weeks before Christmas every year, she puts on her headband and wears it everywhere, spreading Christmas joy with her beautiful radiance and her wonderful sense of humor. She is delightful! And she gets lots of kisses and hugs and smiles.

Do you know where the custom of kissing under the mistletoe came from? It began with the druids in northern Europe. They believed mistletoe had curative powers and could heal lots of things including separation between people. So when two enemies happened to meet under an oak tree with mistletoe hanging above them, they took it as a sign from God that they should drop their weapons and be reconciled. They would set aside their animosities and embrace one another under the mistletoe.

When Christian missionaries moved into northern Europe, they saw this mistletoe custom as a perfect symbol for what happened at Christmas—that Jesus Christ came into the world to save us, to redeem us, and to bring us peace, healing, forgiveness, love, and reconciliation. He came to show us God's love and to show us how to love one another. In a real sense, the Prince of Peace came to show us how to embrace one another, as the druids did, and live together in peace.

If you want to have a "peace-full" Christmas, go in the spirit of love and fix the broken relationships in your life. If you are alienated or estranged or cut off or at odds with any other person, go in the spirit of Christmas and make peace. Don't put it off any longer. Drop your pride, your resentment, your grudges, and go set it right. With the help of God, go make peace today. Christmas offers us the gift of peace with others, but it's up to us to accept that gift.

At Christmas, the Christ Child comes into the world as the Prince of Peace. He brings the peace that passes understanding, the peace that we are called to pass on to others.

Hope. Love. Joy. And Peace.

These are the Christmas gifts that always fit.

These are the Christmas gifts that never go out of style.

These are the Christmas gifts wrapped in heaven.

These are the Christmas gifts that we as Christian disciples are called upon to pass on to others.

These are the Christmas gifts that won't break!

DISCUSSION QUESTIONS

1. Think of times in your life when you needed the gift of peace. Did you receive it? Why or why not?

2. What does it mean to be a peacemaker and to give the gift of peace?

3. During the Christmas season, what are some of the ways in which we receive the gift of peace?

4. What are some of the ways in which we can seek inner peace? Recall and share some of the times when you successfully found inner peace.

5. What factors can prevent us from being at peace with others? List some simple ways to become a more peaceful person.

6. How has this Advent study helped you prepare for Christmas?

PRAYER

Dear God, thank you for the gift of peace. Help us put peace into practice in our lives and show others the path to true peace. Remind us to serve as peacemakers and to share the love of God with those in need. Amen.

FOCUS FOR THE WEEK

Christmas will be here soon. Focus this week on the spirit of the season. Spread gifts of hope, love, joy, and peace to those in need of lasting gifts. Prepare your heart for Christmas and find ways to help others do the same. Live in peace as Christmas draws near.

Devotions
CHAPTER FOUR

YOUR NAME IS PRINTED
IN THE PROGRAM

Luke 2:8-14

When my youngest daughter, Phoebe, was five years old, she was the flower girl in my cousin's wedding. It was a big, fancy wedding. It had it all: expensive dresses, rented tuxedos, beautiful flower arrangements, a nervous groom, a glowing bride. You know, the whole deal. My family of five loaded up in the minivan and made the ten-hour drive to Jacksonville. We had to. Phoebe was the flower girl.

Phoebe was afraid. She doesn't like being in front of people. She won't sing in the children's choir at church. It's just not her thing. At the wedding rehearsal, all of her fears came out in big tears that flowed down her cheeks. She couldn't hold it in; she began to cry audibly. I rescued her from the front of the church and wondered if we had driven down here for a no-show. We had to find some way to convince her to participate. Her name was already printed in the program.

Phoebe's fear was understandable. Let's face it, it is scary to be included in something really big, especially when you feel really small.

On the drive to the church the next night, tears ran down Phoebe's cheeks again. She asked me how many people would be sitting in the congregation. I knew it would be a lot. We arrived and our little flower girl was whisked away to be with the bridal party. When Phoebe walked in, the bride exclaimed, "Phoebe, you look beautiful." Then the bride asked, "Do you think Allen [the groom] will think I'm pretty?" Phoebe nodded. She was a part of this. The bride was asking Phoebe her opinion on important matters. It was a lot to take in.

I sat on the front row, because Phoebe had been told that if she made it down the aisle, she could sit up front with me during the ceremony and then walk out at the end. I sat there as the guests filled the beautiful sanctuary of the historic church. The room filled up, and then the balcony. This is a lot to include a little girl in, I thought. I wondered if she would make it to the front.

She did. She made a fast walk that turned into a run, forgetting to throw any flower petals down, rounded the front pew, and came right to my seat. "You made it!" I whispered. We sat and watched the ceremony. Phoebe was mesmerized.

She sat still and listened to the words and prayers. She seemed to grow in confidence as she realized she had been invited to dress up and be a part of this, to have a crucial role, her name printed in the program. Then the final prayer came. Phoebe stood up as if she knew it was her cue. "It's time Dad," she said. "Yep," I answered. "Are you going to go?" And then I heard "Whooooooosh." Phoebe exhaled a big breath, walked out of my hands to the altar rail at the front, and followed the bride and groom as they walked out to start their lives in the big, crazy world that awaited them outside the doors of the church. Phoebe's walk out was different from her walk in. It was slower and more purposeful. She floated instead of ran. She smiled instead of grimaced. Later, she danced the night away at the reception and fell asleep on her nana's shoulder.

We get used to the idea of Mary, Joseph, and the shepherds being special. Some of us have heard the story so many times that we don't even blink when we hear about the unwed teenage girl's invitation to carry the Son of God in her womb. We have grown accustomed to the thought of Joseph stepping out on faith after only having one crazy dream. We nod along when we hear of the shepherds leaving their post at work to run to town to see a baby king. They are our heroes, and rightly so.

But during Advent this year as we hear the stories again, we are invited to step back and hear them as if for the first time. We are invited to imagine what it must have been like to be included in something so very big when you feel really small.

97

When Elizabeth [that is, Mary's cousin] was six months pregnant, God sent the angel Gabriel to Nazareth, a city in Galilee, to a virgin who was engaged to a man named Joseph, a descendant of David's house. The virgin's name was Mary. When the angel came to her, he said, "Rejoice, favored one! The Lord is with you!" She was confused by these words and wondered what kind of greeting this might be. The angel said, "Don't be afraid, Mary. God is honoring you. Look! You will conceive and give birth to a son, and you will name him Jesus. He will be great and he will be called the Son of the Most High. The Lord God will give him the throne of David his father. He will rule over Jacob's house forever, and there will be no end to his kingdom."

Then Mary said to the angel, "How will this happen since I haven't had sexual relations with a man?"

The angel replied, "The Holy Spirit will come over you and the power of the Most High will overshadow you. Therefore, the one who is to be born will be holy. He will be called God's Son."

(Luke 1:26-35)

Mary was invited into the story. She took a deep breath, exhaled, and walked out to do something big.

As he was thinking about this, an angel from the Lord appeared to him in a dream and said, "Joseph son

*of David, don't be afraid to take Mary as your wife,
because the child she carries was conceived by the
Holy Spirit. She will give birth to a son, and you will
call him Jesus, because he will save his people from
their sins."*

(Matthew 1:20-21)

Joseph was invited into the story. He took a deep breath, exhaled, and walked out to do something big.

*When the angels returned to heaven, the shepherds
said to each other, "Let's go right now to Bethlehem
and see what's happened. Let's confirm what the Lord
has revealed to us."*

(Luke 2:15)

The shepherds were invited into the story. They took a deep breath, exhaled, and walked out to do something big.

Mary, Joseph, and the shepherds were all invited into the story, and they must have been afraid. But they each took a deep breath, exhaled, and walked out to do something that seemed so big and wonderful. They accepted that God was including them in it.

This is what Christmas is about. It's about God coming into the lives of fear-filled people in a fear-filled world and bringing the gift of peace. The peace allows those of us who would have never thought we could be a part of something so big to find our rightful place in the story of God's love for all people. The peace gives us a new walk. We wipe away the tears and walk confidently into the world, because we see just how beautiful it is that God has invited us to be a part of the grand thing God is doing.

Many of us are now in touch with fear and evil in a way that we have never encountered before. Some of us can remember a time during the Advent season many years ago—December 7, 1941—when in a fear-filled world America was brought abruptly into World War II. There was a lot of fear then, tragically causing Japanese Americans to be put in internment camps. Some of us remember what the 1950s and 1960s felt like with the Korean War, the Cuban Missile Crisis, and the Cold War. We remember the kind of fear that led children to get under their desks at school, hands over heads to practice what it would be like if a bomb was dropped. More of us remember Martin Luther King Jr.'s dream for a nation where we could live in harmony no matter the color of our skin. Great strides were made by his and others' heroic work, but still today people live with fear because of the color of their skin. Many more of us remember where we were on September 11, 2001. We have moved on with our lives, but many still live lives filled with the fear of terror attacks. There is still the threat of bombs, more school shootings, more innocent people losing their lives, and children and families running for their lives. Fear is real.

The story of Jesus' birth is precisely for times like this. We have to remember that the Christmas story includes those who are afraid and includes those who are looking for peace. Mary and Joseph with baby Jesus would flee for terror of their lives being taken and become refugees for a time. They didn't understand how they, so small, could be used in something so big. Yet they walked with confidence to do something that could only be done with the Holy Spirit overshadowing them. They experienced peace and brought peace into the world.

God is including you in the story. You have a part. You have a role. God has something for you and something God wants to do with you. Your name is already printed in the program.

It will cause you to be afraid. As we have seen over and over, unless you are totally different from the original characters in the Christmas story, you will be afraid. The thought of God using you (yes you!) will cause you to tremble. Instead of letting the fear drive you further into paralysis, let it confirm that you are being included and find yourself in a long line of those who are afraid.

Jesus brings the gift of peace. A baby in a manger is a gift that gives you peace to take a deep breath and then the courage to exhale and step out.

Followers of Jesus can't be silent during Advent. We have something to say. We can't let a meme or a social media post form how we feel in scary times. We are the ones who must say, "Wait, I know a different story." It sounds crazy to proclaim that God has come into the world. But this is what we believe! We don't have to live in fear of a terrorist group or a political party. We live as those who have encountered peace in Jesus, and we become those who bring the gift of peace to proclaim that a King has been born. We bring peace. We bring it into our families, into our offices, into our social media posts, and into the world. We bring the peace that Jesus brings. We are the ones he is sending.

There is always a time when we think, "I can't do something as big as that. I can't bring peace into the world." Isn't that what Mary wondered? How will this be? She told God why she was unqualified, unprepared, and unsuitable for the task. God reminds her that it will not be something she does on her own, but a work of the Holy Spirit. And then, she looks at it all. She considers the enormity, the beauty, and the absurdity that she would be called to be a part of it. Then she exhales and walks out. So do Joseph and the shepherds. Joseph exhales and walks forward to take Mary as his wife. The shepherds breathe out and run down from the fields to meet Jesus.

Oh, how I wish I could keep Phoebe from fear. But I cannot. I can, though, be one who holds her hand and says, "You can do this." I can speak peace to her until she steps out and walks confidently into the crazy world that needs the peace she carries.

Your name is printed in the program. God is calling you, and it will cause you to be afraid. That is the Christmas story! But that is not the end of the Christmas story. Jesus brings the gift of peace. Breathe in, breathe out, step up, step out.

Day 1

We all feel afraid. But we're in good company. We see in the Advent Scriptures that those whom God calls are not exempt from being afraid. And not only that, they are almost exclusively initially filled with fear! What causes you to be afraid today? How can you take a deep breath in God's presence and offer your fears to God?

Day 2

Mary asked "How?" when she realized God wanted to include her in the story. God says that the Holy Spirit will overshadow her. How does the presence of the Holy Spirit empower you in your life?

Day 3

Our world is filled with many fear-inducing situations and injustices. In what ways can Christians offer the gift of peace to a world that is afraid? In what ways can you give the gift of peace?

Day 4

Followers of Jesus can't be silent during Advent. What do you need to say to someone that would help share the story of Jesus? What part of your story can you share that will help bring hope, joy, and peace to someone else?

Day 5

As we think back on times in history when large groups of people or even nations have felt afraid, we see that fear leads people to act and respond in ways that lead to the harm of others. How does fear inform your life and behavior? What helps you find courage in Christ? How can the peace Christ brings enable you to love instead of fear?

Day 6

God showed up to the shepherds in the midst of their normal day (or night) at work. Imagine God showing up in the midst of your day today. Where would you want to see God today? When would you like to see God? Invite God into your ordinary and extraordinary moments today.

Day 7

As we close this week where we have marveled over God's gift of peace to us through Jesus, think of an intentional way that you can share peace. Look for an opportunity where you can share peace with those who may find themselves afraid. In doing so, you will be a part of the story of Christ's coming.

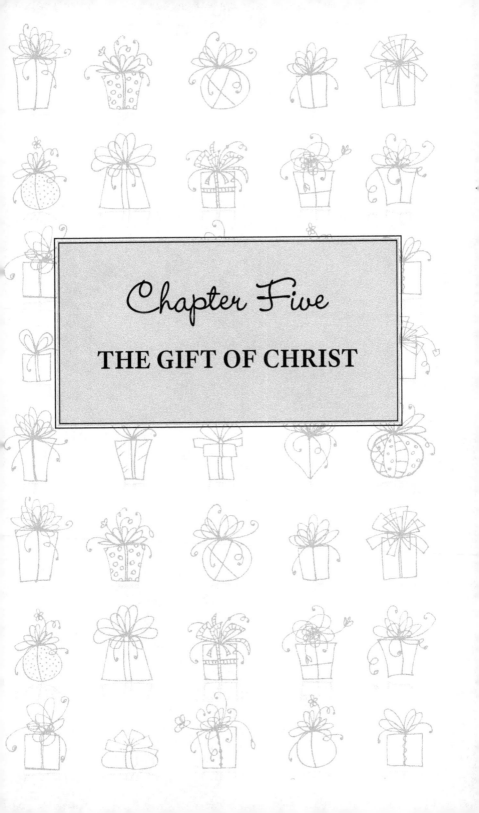

Chapter Five

THE GIFT OF CHRIST

5

THE GIFT OF CHRIST

When they heard the king, they went; and look, the
star they had seen in the east went ahead of them until
it stood over the place where the child was. When they
saw the star, they were filled with joy. They entered the
house and saw the child with Mary his mother. Falling
to their knees, they honored him. Then they opened
their treasure chests and presented him with gifts of
gold, frankincense, and myrrh.

Matthew 2:9-11

Have you ever had a "reality check?" I had one on a Sunday morning several years ago. Right after the 8:30 service in our church's sanctuary, I rushed up to the second floor to get something I needed for the 9:45 service. I went up the stairs in an area called the Commons to a long corridor that led down to the Youth Chapel. About fifty yards up ahead of me, our young people were gathered together out in the hallway, as they do every Sunday morning, visiting and waiting for Sunday School to start.

When I was about forty yards away from them, I saw all of these vivacious students turn and look my way. Suddenly, their faces lit up; they pointed in my direction. They squealed with delight, and then they all started running toward me, smiling warmly, with their arms extended. And I thought: "Isn't that great? Our young people are so good to me. They are always so glad to see me, but today they are really excited. They are just running toward me to give me a big group hug!" So, I smiled back at them and extended my arms, waiting for their hug.

But then, all of a sudden, they just ran right past me on either side! I turned around to see two of our college guys behind me. Jack and Sam had come home for the holidays, and the girls were rushing to hug them, not me! And really, who could blame them for that?

It was a "reality check" for me, and also a valuable life-lesson. The experience reminded me that sometimes, we misread things. Sometimes we misunderstand things. Sometimes we misinterpret things. Sometimes, maybe much of the time, we do that with Christmas: We misread and misunderstand what it's really all about. Before we know it, Christmas has passed us by, and we have missed its warm embrace once again. What we need is a "reality check," to remind us of what Christmas truly means.

Throughout Advent, we have celebrated the Christmas gifts that won't break represented by the outer candles of the Advent wreath: hope, love, joy, and peace. Now, we celebrate the greatest gift of all, represented by the center candle: the gift of Jesus Christ. Jesus really is what it's all about, what Christmas truly means.

Each year on Thanksgiving Day, as our family sits down for our Thanksgiving feast, we pray our prayer of gratitude and then we go around the table to say what we are thankful for. Each member of the family expresses what she or he is especially grateful for this year.

One year when we did this, our family members mentioned family, friends, food...and my wife June's good results from her chemotherapy. We got all the way around the table and finally, our granddaughter Sarah was the last one. She always rises to the occasion and never ceases to surprise. She said, "I'm thankful for Mimi, for family, for friends, for food, and for those world-famous words, 'Let's Dig In!'"

Well, actually that's what the season of Advent is for. It helps us to "dig into" the real truth of Christmas, and get ourselves prepared and ready for a joyous and meaningful celebration of Christmas.

So let's dig in—let's celebrate the best Christmas gift of all, the gift of Christ. And, of course, the best place to find Christ is in Bethlehem. So, let's go with the wise men to Bethlehem.

But before we go, we need to be reminded of something that is very important, namely this: there is really only one way to go to Bethlehem. "You have to go on your knees!"

Max Lucado in his book *The Applause of Heaven* puts it like this:

> A small cathedral outside Bethlehem marks the supposed birthplace of Jesus. Behind the high altar in the church is a cave, a little cavern lit by silver lamps. You can enter the main edifice and admire the ancient church. You can also enter the quiet cave where a star embedded in the floor recognizes the birth of the King. There is

one stipulation, however. You have to stoop. The door is so low you can't go in standing up.

The same is true of the Christ. You can see the world standing tall, but to witness the Savior, you have to get on your knees.

So...while the theologians were sleeping and the elite were dreaming and the successful were snoring, the meek were kneeling. They were kneeling before the One only the meek will see. They were kneeling in front of Jesus.[1]

So, now in the spirit of humility and in the spirit of expectancy, let us go over to Bethlehem and honor the newborn King. Let us go see and celebrate the gift of Christ. And let me suggest three things that I'm sure we will find there, three things we can expect the gift of Christ to bring us.

THE GIFT OF CHRIST BRINGS US THE GIFT OF FAITH

Some years ago, I was privileged to go with a tour group to the Holy Land. I will never forget that morning when we came to the church at Bethlehem. It was such a thrill for me to come to that sacred place where Jesus Christ was born.

An old man, who was a native of Bethlehem, was standing there in front of the church that marks the spot of Christ's birth. As we walked toward the church, he watched us. Suddenly, he waved to me to get my attention and he said, "Are you an American?"

"Yes," I answered.

"Are you a Christian?" he asked.

"Yes!" I said.

He reached over and took my hand in his. He smiled warmly and said, "Welcome Home! Welcome Home!"

He was right, you know. He was right. Bethlehem is the birthplace, the home of our faith. It was there that we first received the Christ Child. It was there that the drama of redemption took a dramatic turn. It was there that God came to visit and redeem God's people. The gift of Jesus Christ is the gift of the very foundation of our faith.

The Olympic Games always produce a number of dramatic and memorable moments. One of the most touching and poignant of all time occurred in the Olympics at Barcelona in 1992. Perhaps you saw it on TV or read about it.

This particular moment happened during the semifinals of the men's 400-meter race. Great Britain's Derek Redmond went down on the backstretch with a torn hamstring. Despite the excruciating pain, the injured runner struggled to his feet, fended off medical attendants who had rushed out to help him . . . and he started to hop on one leg in a determined effort to finish the race.

When he reached the stretch, a large man in a T-shirt emerged out of the stands. He pushed his way through the security guards and ran to Derek Redmond and hugged him. It was Derek Redmond's father. "You don't have to do this," he told his weeping son.

"Yes, I do," whispered Derek through his pain.

"Well, then," said the father, "we're going to finish this together."

So they did. Waving away the security guards and the medical helpers, the son's head sometimes buried in his father's shoulder, the two men stayed in Derek's lane and crossed the finish line. The crowd watched, then rose, then cheered, then wept.

It's a great parable for Christmas, isn't it? Realizing that we can't make it, that we are down and out, that we need help, God sends us a Savior. In Jesus Christ, God comes into our world (into our arena) to pick us up, to hold us up, to see us through, and to bring us home.

This is the faith of Christmas: "God so loved the world that he gave his only Son, so that everyone who believes in him won't perish but will have eternal life" (John 3:16).

That's the first thing: Let us go over to Bethlehem and receive the gift of faith, the gift that Christ brings to us.

THE GIFT OF CHRIST BRINGS US THE GIFT OF HOPE

Several years ago, a small town called Hope, Alaska, was destroyed by a flood. No lives were lost, but there was tremendous property damage. A bishop went there to see how he might help. When he arrived, he found the devastated town completely deserted. However, someone had placed a small sign in the center of what had once been the main street of the little town. The sign said:

The Community of Hope Has Moved to Higher Ground.

This is what the miracle of Christmas, the gift of Christ, does for us. It moves our hope to higher ground. It reminds us of the power and love of God. It reminds us that God is indeed the King of Kings, the Prince of Peace, the Lord of Heaven and Earth—and that God cannot be defeated.

Even though evil will sometimes make loud noises in our world, as Christians we can be confident. We can be filled with hope because we know that ultimately God and righteousness will win. And just think of it: God wants to share the victory with us. That's why the Christ Child came into the world...to bring the good news of God's ultimate victory. That is our hope.

The great hymn writer Charles Wesley expresses it powerfully like this:

> Hark! the herald angels sing,
> "Glory to the newborn King;
> peace on earth, and mercy mild,
> God and sinners reconciled!"
>
> Joyful, all ye nations rise,
> Join the triumph of the skies;
> with th'angelic host proclaim,
> "Christ is born in Bethlehem!"
>
> Hark! the herald angels sing,
> "Glory to the newborn King!"[2]

Our hope is one that will see God and sinners reconciled, with peace on earth and all people praising God's glory. At Bethlehem, in Christ, we find faith and hope.

THE GIFT OF CHRIST BRINGS US THE GIFT OF LOVE

And we find love. "Love came down at Christmas." That's the way we sing it, and appropriately so. Most of all, Christmas is about love. The gift of Christ is the very gift of love itself coming to be with us.

In his book *Solid Living in a Shattered World*, Bill Hinson told about a Christmas several years ago when his daughter, Cathy, received a perky little white puppy for Christmas. Cathy noticed that the little dog constantly wagged his tail vigorously, so she decided to name him "Happy" because she said he has such a happy ending!

It became Dad's job to build a doghouse for Happy, but when the new house was completed, Happy wanted no part of it. It was too dark, too big, too foreboding. The little white puppy named Happy would not go near the doghouse. When they would pick him up and put him in, he would run immediately out, trembling and scared to death. They tried everything—warnings, pleadings, commands, threats, bribes—but to no avail. Nothing worked. Happy would not go into the new doghouse. He was terrified of it.

Finally, Bill said he gave up in frustration and went into the parsonage to get a drink of water. As he looked out the kitchen window, he couldn't believe his eyes. He saw Happy, with tail wagging joyously, trot right into the doghouse and lie down serenely.

He was amazed. What an incredible change! How could this happen? He went out to investigate.

You know what he found, don't you? His daughter, little Cathy, had crawled into the doghouse and was resting inside. When Happy saw Cathy go inside, he trotted right in there beside her and made it his home!

The point is clear: Where all those other things had failed, love prevailed. That's what Christmas teaches us. Love is the single most powerful thing in the world. And in the gift of Christ, we receive the gift of love in the most powerful and perfect way.

The wise men came to Bethlehem to honor Jesus with three gifts.

When we go to Bethlehem we receive three gifts, I'm sure of it:

The miracle of Christmas Faith!

The miracle of Christmas Hope!

And, the miracle of Christmas Love!

And most of all, we receive the one true gift that makes faith, hope, and love possible: the gift of Jesus Christ, the gift of a Savior!

DISCUSSION QUESTIONS

1. In order to go to Bethlehem, you have to go "on your knees." How do you need to humble yourself in order to experience the newborn Jesus?

2. In what way do you feel the need for a Savior right now? How does the birth of Jesus give you faith that God is on your side?

3. What do you tend to put your hope in? What dangers lie in hoping in worldly things?

4. How can the gift of Christ elevate your hope? What will change by moving your hope to higher ground?

5. How will love prevail in your life? What does God's love make possible for you?

PRAYER

Dear God, we celebrate the unbreakable Christmas gifts of hope, love, joy, and peace. And most of all, we celebrate the greatest gift, Jesus Christ, your Son who came to be with us. We know that because you are here, our very lives are renewed. Give us the wisdom and courage to put these unbreakable gifts to work in our lives throughout the coming year, knowing that you are with us always. Amen.

FOCUS FOR THE WEEK

The gift of Jesus Christ is a gift for all people. This week, tell someone about the good news of Jesus Christ and what it has meant in your life. Pray for that person, and ask God to help them experience the good news as well.

1   Max Lucado: , *The Applause of* Heaven: *Discover the Secret to a Truly Satisfying Life* (Nashville: Thomas Nelson, 2011), 75–76.
2   Charles Wesley, "Hark! the Herald Angels Sing," *The United Methodist Hymnal* (Nashville: Abingdon, 1989), 240.

Devotions
CHAPTER FIVE

WE STILL NEED JESUS

Matthew 2:1-12

It was an ordinary Tuesday morning during Advent when I dropped my girl off at the school and arrived at the gym with the best of intentions. I stepped onto the treadmill and set off at a tired Tuesday-morning pace. My attention was quickly caught by the bank of TVs that are above the rows of treadmills. My eyes were taken to a breaking-news banner on the TV screen. There had been a terrible massacre of innocent people halfway around the world in the Middle East. While I had been sleeping, unsuspecting men, women, and children had lost their lives. I took a breath and wiped the sleep out of my eyes. I stopped the treadmill as images began to pop up on the screen of wounded children. Before I could even think about this tragedy, a moving crawler on the bottom of the screen reported a school shooting that had broken out in a neighboring state. And then, almost at the same time, my phone buzzed with a message giving details for the memorial service for a beloved teacher in our community who had died after a valiant fight with cancer.

I wanted to take my earbuds out, close my eyes, and throw my phone across the room. But I know as well as you do that closing your ears and eyes is not enough to shut out the pain of this world. All of this was happening in the week leading up to Christmas. On a week when it seemed every night I would put on holiday clothes and head to some type of Christmas celebration, all of this pain and loss was going on in the world around me.

The Scripture from Matthew 2 tells the classic story of three wise men traveling a far distance, following a star to come to a place where the Christ Child dwelled. They brought gifts of gold, frankincense, and myrrh. You have likely heard the story before. After Jesus was born in Bethlehem, during the time of King Herod, magi, or wise men, who were sort of king priests of a different religion in Persia, came to Jerusalem and asked, "Where is the newborn king of the Jews? We've seen his star in the east, and we've come to honor him" (Matthew 2:2).

We then customarily skip down a few verses and read the part about how a star stopped over the place where Jesus was, and the magi bowed down and gave gifts and worshiped him. It is a beautiful scene in our beautiful story. Even though the timing is probably a bit off, we show the scene in our Nativity sets.

But this is not the whole story. Matthew 2 tells us that King Herod becomes greatly disturbed when he hears that these three seeming kings have come all that way looking for a new king. King Herod is the Roman-appointed ruler of the Jews, so when three rich foreigners travel for months to welcome a new king of the Jews, he is more than a bit bothered. Herod calls together his chief priests and professors and says in effect, "Hey, I know we have been awaiting a Messiah. I know we long for a new king to save us from all of our brokenness and sin. Just curious, where do the ancient texts say that will happen?" (see Matthew 2:4). The chief priests and scribes open up their ancient scrolls and say:

In Bethlehem of Judea, for this is what the prophet wrote:

> You, Bethlehem, land of Judah,
>> by no means are you least among the
>> rulers of Judah,
>>> because from you will come one
>>> who governs,
>>> who will shepherd my people
>>> Israel.
>>>> *(Matthew 2:5-6)*

Upon hearing this, Herod sends the wise men to Bethlehem to find this new king and report back. He does this because he wants to kill the new king.

After meeting Jesus and Mary and Joseph, though, the wise men don't go back to Herod. Matthew says, "They went back to their own country by another route" (Matthew 2:12). They didn't get a good vibe from King Herod, so they went home a different way.

And then in the same chapter of Matthew—where we read of the birth of Jesus, right there in our story—it says, "When Herod knew the magi had fooled him, he grew very angry. He sent soldiers to kill all the children in Bethlehem and in all the surrounding territory who were two years old and younger, according to the time that he had learned from the magi" (Matthew 2:16).

The first Christmas took place at a time in the world when innocent children were killed.

The first Christmas took place at a time when evil people did evil things.

The first Christmas took place in a week when the community cried together.

We need to hear our story again. We need to hear the whole story, and we need Christ to come again. Nativity scenes are beautiful; we usually have several set up in our home during the Christmas season. But Jesus came into a world that desperately needed not just a beautiful scene, but a beautiful savior.

At Christmas we often want to tell a pretty story that gives us warm feelings, and certainly Christmas does that. But if you lived in the real world this week, where innocent children were killed, where evil people did evil things, where communities cry together, then you know we need to hear our story again. We need to hear the whole story with all its ugly details. We need the gift of Jesus to come into our lives again.

122

Our story starts in a garden where God made us in God's image. There was life. There was love. There was relationship. God was so close that God came and walked with Adam in the afternoon. Then the people in the garden did what we did today and yesterday, and what we will do tomorrow. They chose to take hold of the thing God said not to take hold of. Sin entered into the world, and the people were cast out of the garden. They were cast out into a world where everything was not right.

But our story tells us that God still came after them over and over again.

One of the first things that people did was to make sacrifices to God in the hopes of making things right. The first children ever, Cain and Abel, offered sacrifices from the best of the field and the best of the flock. Sacrifices were made to try and make things better, to try and make a way back. The sacrifices were pleasing to God, but they never seemed to be enough.

God made a promise to Abraham that he would make his descendants as numerous as the stars of the sky. Pay no mind that he was one hundred years old and his wife ninety before they had the child of the covenant, Isaac. God fulfilled the promise. And Isaac was the first of Abraham's many descendants who would become the people of Israel. But those descendants continued the legacy of taking hold of what God said don't take hold of. They continued the legacy of sin. And all the while, God continued God's legacy of coming after them over and over again.

123

Some generations later, those same people found themselves enslaved. God heard their cry, and God delivered them from slavery. They were cast out into the wilderness for a long time. There they offered sacrifice after sacrifice trying to make things right. Finally, they were led into the Promised Land. They hadn't been there long, though, until the people cried out for a king. God told them that they didn't need a king. God was their king. They insisted that they wanted a human king. Again, God tried to tell them the problems that come with human kings. They demanded a human king.

Well, they got their human king, and the great human king experiment went poorly. It started with the very first one. There were some good kings in the bunch of kings that came after, but mostly the kings led the people to take hold of what God said don't take hold of. The people turned their backs on God. The people made sacrifice after sacrifice.

We usually read the pretty parts of our story, especially at Christmas. But our story, the story of God's people, includes many stories of innocent people being treated unfairly, of evil people doing evil things, and of communities crying together. Really, if anything, that's our story. The people come together and cry before God in a broken world.

The people of God longed for, waited for, ached for this one thing God said God would do: send a Savior, save their story.

As we fast-forward, we arrive at some wise men who follow a star because they believe where it leads them is to this long-awaited One. Understandably, they go to the king first. They can tell, though, that he doesn't know what's going on.

124

They make their way to find an unsuspecting couple with a baby boy. They fall down on their knees and give him gifts.

Gold. This is what you give a king. The people asked for a king a long time ago, and even though God told them they didn't want a human king, they demanded one and got one. In Jesus, God becomes the king once again. The wise men represent how people from all the world will acknowledge this baby boy as the true king. **They brought gold, the gift for a king.**

Frankincense. For centuries incense had been used in the temple to symbolize the prayers of the people going up. The burning incense was a way of seeing the longing of the people going up to God. Zechariah the priest had carried on this tradition of coming before God on behalf of the people of God, lighting the incense and lifting it up to God. The magi knew about the role of the priest. Jesus was the priest who could make a way for the longings of the people to meet with God. **They brought frankincense, the gift for a priest.**

Myrrh. Myrrh was used to embalm and prepare dead bodies for burial. This is a strange gift for a baby boy. It is strange unless you understand that for centuries the people have faced death and destruction. It is strange unless you remember that for generations people have made sacrifices to God. Jesus would be the final sacrifice, once for all. **They brought myrrh, the gift for a funeral.**

125

In Jesus, God unwraps the gift that we all need. The Christmas story is about a broken world where the innocents' innocence is taken away, where evil things happen, where communities cry together—where God comes. Jesus is for communities where beloved teachers die too early. He is for places where schoolchildren are not safe. He is for places where people live in terror.

Jesus comes as the one true King. Jesus comes as priest to make a way for us to be close to God and to one another, like it was in the garden. Jesus comes to die. Jesus comes to die the death that we can't die, so that we can live the life we can only have in him.

Jesus comes as a baby. If Herod had remembered the story, he would have known that the prophets said a child would be born and the government would be upon his shoulders. He would be called "Wonderful Counselor, Mighty God, / Eternal Father, [and] Prince of Peace" (Isaiah 9:6). Isaiah also wrote that the Messiah King would be rejected and despised, that he would be familiar with pain. Isaiah wrote that he would take up our pain and bear our sufferings. The King's punishment would bring us peace and by his wounds we would find healing (Isaiah 52:13–53:12).

The gift of Christ is the gift of hope, love, joy, and peace for the whole world.

Day 1

We live in a world filled with injustice, terror, and tears. We know that this is also precisely the kind of world to which the Christ Child entered. How does this inform and empower how you see our world today?

Day 2

The wise men traveled a long way so they could bow before and worship the Christ Child. In the midst of all the busy-ness and movement of the Christmas season, where could you travel today to bow before and worship Jesus?

Day 3

As we have seen, the gift of Jesus brings hope, peace, joy, and love. Which of these is most needed in your life today? Is there something else that Jesus brings that you are longing for?

Day 4

With the gift of gold, the wise men acknowledged Jesus as King. How do you experience Jesus as King in your life? How can you honor Jesus as the one true King?

Day 5

With the gift of frankincense, the wise men brought to mind the centuries of incense that had been used in the temple as a sign of prayers being lifted to God. The gift of incense helps us see Jesus as priest, one who brings our longings to the throne of God. What prayers, what longings would you lift to God today?

Day 6

With the gift of myrrh, the wise men remind us that Jesus' life and death are of great importance to us. What does Jesus' death mean to you? How does Jesus' death inform how you see death?

Day 7

As we close this week where we have marveled over God's great gift of Jesus to us, think of an intentional way that you can share Christ with someone. Look for an opportunity where you can share Jesus and in doing so, you will be a part of the story of Christ's coming.